Change Everything Now

A Selection of Essays
from Orion *Magazine*

ORION

Orion Readers are published by *Orion* magazine.
All essays appeared in *Orion*.

Orion
187 Main Street, Great Barrington, Massachusetts 01230
Telephone: 888/909-6568
Fax: 413/528-0676
www.orionmagazine.org

Design by Hans Teensma/Impress

Cover photograph by Brandon Hill, www.storyofb.com

This volume was made possible by generous support from The Clements Foundation.

ISBN (print): 978-1-935713-00-5

ISBN (e-book): 978-1-935713-01-2

In memory of Robert Clements

CONTENTS

FOREWORD

IT'S IMPORTANT to take time out to lie on your back in the grass, looking for shapes in the clouds, to cultivate contentment, give yourself to the moment, unplug. In fact you'd darn well better, because as soon as something pulls you out of your reverie, there are alarm bells ringing in every corner. Things are going terribly wrong in the twenty-first century. The litany of distressing problems is formidable, the sense of urgency real. There is fear for what the future might bring, or not bring. There is the pressing feeling that we're going to be in big trouble if we don't change everything now.

Because in order to be solutions, solutions have to actually fix things, and much of what passes for fixing today is completely out of scale with the level of change needed. If you believe in tipping points, then you are probably among those who wake in the night, worrying about the *when?* *how?* and the *then what?* Perhaps at times you've been called Chicken Little, or accused of having a glass-half-empty mindset. But more often than not it feels as if the glass is not just half empty, but getting emptier day by day.

This is not a moment for timidity. It is not a time for cowardice. We must be bold in the face of what our era demands of us. Unless there is a huge cultural shift in the very near future, things could get very bad for people and the planet—that is the message of the essays collected here. The point is not to belittle small acts, but let's not fool ourselves into thinking that they can add up to what's needed now.

In 1982, when *Orion* made its debut, there was no shortage of ecological problems to illuminate through thoughtful magazine writing. But thirty years on, the situation is greatly compounded. Much has happened. We've learned more about precisely what has happened, is happening, will continue to happen. And thus a new art form has evolved: the literature of ecological urgency. Ranging from the stern to the satirical, the essays in this volume are unapologetic. They ask us to fundamentally change the way we view the world we are living in. They ask us to live as if our lives really do matter, to assume a whole new level of responsibility for the kind of world we will leave behind.

Be forewarned: there are plenty of inconvenient truths in these pages. Among the "solutions" that are deemed insufficient herein are taking shorter showers, driving hybrid cars, buying BPA-free water bottles, and using cloth napkins. Among the things we must now put on our to-do list are exterminating consumerism, overhauling environmentalism, restoring social and economic equity, punishing corporate polluters, and revoking the laws that give them permission to poison people and the land.

It's hard not to feel overwhelmed as the daily e-mails roll in—help the manatee, stop the pipeline, protest the dictatorship, support the cleanup. There's scarcely time to read them all, let alone money enough to support all this very good work. But some solace can be found in the realization that our problems are more systemic than any single species, corporation, nation, or candidate for office. Big change is what's needed, and our agenda must reflect this. The challenge is ours to embrace.

Of course, a collection of essays alone will not bring about cultural change. But few movements have been born that did not have an associated literature to buoy them. Consider this book a roadmap of sorts, a declaration of the scale on which we must operate if we are to set course for a promising future.

JENNIFER SAHN
Editor, *Orion*

Change
Everything
Now

JEFF GOODELL

CHANGE EVERYTHING NOW

An interview with James Gustave Speth

JAMES GUSTAVE "GUS" SPETH'S OFFICE at Yale reeks of Old World charm, with a high ceiling and dark, wood-paneled walls adorned with souvenirs from his travels in Africa and Asia. Speth, sixty-six, the dean of the Yale School of Forestry and Environmental Studies, is a tall, genial man who wears conservative striped ties and speaks in a quiet southern drawl. If America can be said to have a distinguished elder statesman of environmental policy, Speth is it. Before he arrived at Yale, he cofounded the Natural Resources Defense Council, one of the most powerful environmental groups in the U.S., then went on to serve as a top environmental policy advisor to President Jimmy Carter. In 1982, he founded the World Resources Institute, an environmental think tank, which he headed for a decade. He also served as a senior advisor to President-elect Bill Clinton's transition team and spent seven years as the top administrator in the Development Programme at the United Nations.

It's not surprising that Speth would end up in a wood-paneled office at Yale. What is surprising, however, is that he uses his bully pulpit in academia to push for a 1960s-style take-it-to-the-streets revolution. His new book, *The Bridge at the Edge of the World* (Yale University Press), is nothing less than a call for an uprising that would reinvent modern capitalism and replace it with, well, a postmodern capitalism that values sustainability over growth, and doing good over making a quick buck. Sound idealistic? It is—but that's part of the book's appeal. Speth goes beyond finger-wagging to indict consumer capitalism itself for the rape and pillage of the natural world. His proximate concern is global warming and the impact it will have on civilized life as we know it. But unlike, say, Al Gore, Speth is not concerned with details of climate science or policy prescriptions for the near-term. He is after bigger game—the Wal-Martization of America, our slavish devotion to an ever-expanding gross domestic product, the utter failure of what Speth disparagingly calls "modern capitalism" to create a sustainable world. What is needed, Speth believes, is not simply a tax on greenhouse gas emissions, but "a new operating system" for the modern world.

I spoke with Speth at Yale earlier this year.

JEFF GOODELL: *In the opening chapter of your new book, you say, quite bluntly, that "something is wrong" in America. What exactly do you mean?*

GUS SPETH: Well, I think we have to face up to the paradox that while the environmental community has become stronger and more sophisticated over the years, the environment is going downhill so fast that we're facing a potential calamity down the road. All we have to do to leave a ruined world to children is just keep doing what we're doing today—the same emissions of pollutants, the same destruction of ecosystems, the same toxification of the environment—and we'll ruin the planet in the latter part of this century.

And yet, we know we're not just going to keep doing what we're doing. We're going to grow phenomenally. At the current rates, the world economy will be twice as big as it is today in seventeen years. That carries the potential for enormous additional destruction. The environmental movement has a lot of wonderful things about it, and it's accomplished a lot. But it's not up to this challenge of dealing with this amount of environmental loss and destruction.

The fundamental thing that's happened is that our efforts to clean up the environment are being overwhelmed by the sheer increase in the size of the economy. And there's no reason to think that won't continue. So we have to ask, what is it about our society that puts such an extraordinary premium on growth? Is it justified? Why is that growth so destructive? And what do we do about it?

Capitalism is a growth machine. What it really cares about is earning a profit and reinvesting a large share of that and growing continually. Profits can be enhanced if the companies are not paying for the cost of their environmental destruction—so they fight [paying it] tooth and nail. The companies themselves are now quite huge, quite powerful, quite global, and no longer just the main economic actors in our society. They are the main political actors also.

And so all of these things combine to produce a type of capitalism that really doesn't care about the environment, and doesn't really care about people much either. What it really cares about is profits and growth, and the rest is more or less incidental. And until we change that system, my conclusion is that it will continue to be fundamentally destructive.

JG: *So our engine of progress has become the engine of our destruction?*

GS: Well, it's certainly the engine of environmental destruction. And what is also becoming apparent is that this so-called engine of progress is also not really improving people's lives very much either. And here I'm speaking entirely of the advanced, industrial, affluent societies, not the developing world, which does need to grow.

In the West, we're seeing that people's own sense of subjective well-being has not been going up with all of this growth that we've been experiencing. Per capita income goes up, but happiness doesn't, satisfaction with life doesn't. It's just flatlined, for decades now. And there are certain pathologies that have increased. A sense of loneliness in our society, bipolar disorders, other problems, stress and disintegration of communities.

This should be a time when we really can take this fabulous amount of wealth that we've generated and enjoy it, and yet we seem to be caught in a system where it's either up, up, and away or down, down, and out. And we seem to career from crisis to crisis—personal crises, national crises, economic crises.

JG: *I know lots of people working on clean energy technology in places like Silicon Valley who would argue that the forces of progress need to be accelerated, not slowed down.*

GS: Well, I do stress the need to ditch the old technologies that have gotten us into this trouble and bring on as fast as possible new technologies that are designed with the environment in mind. That's all accurate, I think. And I'm delighted to see the renaissance of environmental concern in the country.

But having said that, I just don't believe it's enough. What you're really describing is what can be thought of as kind of a dematerialization of the economy, of the movement toward every kind of gloriously high-tech economy with just electrons moving around—

JG: *A Google economy.*

GS: Yes, a Google economy. But there are still huge impacts, even with all of that, and as these new companies grow in size, those impacts become ever larger. And right now there's been very little dematerialization of the U.S. economy. It's gotten more efficient, it creates less pollutant per unit of output in our economy. But still, we're using a huge amount of stuff and releasing almost all of it back as waste into the environment in some form.

Changes of the type that would bring on this technological nirvana are just too slow and too partial. They need to be combined with other things that basically slow the current up. And that means taking the priority off of growth. It means finding a new set of laws for corporations—to change their incentive structure. It means us consumers becoming more interested in living more simply.

JG: *Of course, when you talk about taking the priority off growth, it's no longer a technological issue. It's a political one.*

GS: Yes, but the trouble is, our politics simply won't sustain the changes that we need. And so we really need to create a mighty force in our country that seeks to reassert popular control over our politics before it's too late.

We're in a vicious circle where the more powerful [certain] interests get, the less able we are to reassert control, and those that have enormous power and wealth in the country [become even more] able to assert even more. And I think that the environmental community needs to see political reform as central to its agenda, and it doesn't now. That's not what the environmental groups do. And that's a huge mistake, because right now they're playing a loser's game, and they keep losing. Winning some battles, but losing the planet.

The other thing that needs to happen is that there needs to be some fundamental challenge to our dominant values. It's been addressed by religious organizations and psychologists and philosophers and countless others for a long time. But until we reconnect in a more profound way with ourselves and our communities and the natural world, it seems unlikely that we will deal successfully with our problems.

JG: *You quote Milton Friedman as saying, "Only a crisis produces real change." What kind of crisis do you have in mind?*

GS: I hope it doesn't take that. But I think if you have a crisis—a Great Depression, whatever—in a time of wise leadership, we can construct a new narrative that builds on the traditions of the country and its highest values, but also explains where we need to go in the future, and why we went astray in the past.

In the end, the thing that I hope for is a huge mass movement in the country before it's too late. I really don't know any other way to make the change happen other than a grassroots movement. The nearest thing we've seen to this in living memory was the civil rights movement.

JG: *One of the paradoxes of this is that fear is not always a good motivator, especially when it comes to confronting an issue like global warming. People become immobilized and say, "What the hell, there's no point." How do you communicate the seriousness of the challenge we face without pushing people over into despair?*

GS: I think people respond out of love and out of fear, fundamentally. We will never do the things that we need to do unless we understand how serious the situation is. So you've got to deal with the facts.

Do we need also to talk in positive terms, to say we can deal with these issues? Absolutely. And is being hopeful about the prospects for the future very important? Absolutely. But in order to make the deep changes that are needed, people need to sense the scale of the problem.

JG: *Do you think the notion of sustainability on a planet that is heading toward 9 billion people is an impossible goal?*

GS: Well, let me give you a personal example. My wife and I have offset all of our greenhouse gas emissions from our car, our house, everything. Before we moved into the apartment where we live now, we invested heavily in a big photovoltaic unit for our house, which produced about half of our electricity. I purchased two Priuses, gave one of them to one of my children. We do lots of recycling and other things. We've changed all our bulbs to CFLs. You do all those things, and your environmental footprint is still huge.

Moreover, not only is doing all the things that we are able to do ourselves woefully insufficient, it creates this false impression. It gives you the sense that the problem is an individual one, and it's on you, and you can solve the problem. Whereas the problem is really deeply systemic—it's only through political action that we will solve the problem.

JG: *I visited scientist James Lovelock a few months ago, who has long argued that the Earth is beyond its carrying capacity for human beings. He basically says, "Look, if there were 100 million people on the planet, it wouldn't matter if we were all driving SUVs and burning coal—"*

GS: And it almost wouldn't matter if we were back in 1950, with half the population that we have now. It still wasn't a full world at that point. Now it is a full world. Everything we're doing is on a scale that rivals the natural systems.

JG: *Right. And you can say—as you do—that we consume too much, and that our economic system has become a slave to the idea of an ever-expanding GDP. But you could also just say, "Look, there are too many people on the planet—"*

GS: Well, I think a lot of people believe that. I actually have a law, Speth's Law, and it is that the richer you are, the more you think that population is the world's problem.

But the scale of the impact is really derived from the phenomenal amount of economic growth in rich countries, not from the phenomenal population growth.

JG: *In your view, what's the alternative to pro-growth capitalism? Should we rethink communism?*

GS: No, it's not that at all. But I do believe we should be looking for a nonsocialist alternative to today's capitalism. I think we do want to make changes that are sufficiently profound that when you look back on them, you will see that it's no longer the capitalism of the early twenty-first century.

JG: *What would a revised capitalist system look like?*

GS: Well, let's take the core of it—the corporation. Corporations right now are mandated to serve and promote the best interest of stockholders, by law. And anything it [a corporation] justifies in the nature of doing well in communities or doing well by society, that's also got to be justified that it's in the best interest of the shareholders. And maximizing shareholder wealth is a very fundamental part of the motivational structure of the corporate sector.

I think that needs to change fundamentally, so that corporations really are in the business of serving all of the factors that help generate wealth—all of the stakeholders, in effect.

One way to describe what has to happen, and the way that the situation in the future would be different, would be to describe it as a series of transformations. The first would be a transformation in the market. There would be a real revolution in pricing. Things that are environmentally destructive would be—if they were really destructive—almost out of reach, prohibitively expensive.

A second would be a transformation to a postgrowth society where what you really want is to grow very specific things that are desperately needed in a very targeted way—you know, care for the mentally ill, health-care accessibility, high-tech green-collar industries.

A third would be a move to a wider variety of ownership patterns in the private sector. More co-ops, more employee ownership plans, and less rigid lines between the profit and the not-for-profit sectors. I mean, Google is an example of that now, they are moving in that direction, although I think it's small compared with what they've really got going.

JG: *Do you think that this kind of change can be had with anything short of a real revolution in America?*

GS: Well, I don't think it can be had without a real citizens' movement—a grassroots citizens' movement that shakes up people's consciousness and forces us to rethink what's really important, and what our role in the world and in nature really is. I think there is a growing sense that something is out of whack in the country, and that we're on the verge of losing something very important, not only spiritually but also environmentally. And if we don't change, we really could pass into some situation where it would be irretrievably lost.

JG: *If I read your book right, you stop just short of calling for people to march in the streets.*

GS: Oh, I will call for people to march in the streets. I said to my friend Laurie David [producer of *An Inconvenient Truth*] that it's time for a million-person march on Washington early in the new administration. We could really make the point that the climate issue has to be front and center in the first hundred days of the new administration. It's amazing what can be accomplished if citizens are to march in the footsteps of Dr. King. It's time to give the world a sense of hope again.

(2008)

JEFFREY KAPLAN

THE GOSPEL OF CONSUMPTION

And the better future we left behind

PRIVATE CARS were relatively scarce in 1919 and horse-drawn conveyances were still common. In residential districts, electric streetlights had not yet replaced many of the old gaslights. And within the home, electricity remained largely a luxury item for the wealthy.

Just ten years later things looked very different. Cars dominated the streets and most urban homes had electric lights, electric flat irons, and vacuum cleaners. In upper-middle-class houses, washing machines, refrigerators, toasters, curling irons, percolators, heating pads, and popcorn poppers were becoming commonplace. And although the first commercial radio station didn't begin broadcasting until 1920, the American public, with an adult population of about 122 million people, bought 4,438,000 radios in the year 1929 alone.

But despite the apparent tidal wave of new consumer goods and what appeared to be a healthy appetite for their consumption among the well-to-do, industrialists were worried. They feared that the frugal habits maintained by most

American families would be difficult to break. Perhaps even more threatening was the fact that the industrial capacity for turning out goods seemed to be increasing at a pace greater than people's sense that they needed them.

It was this latter concern that led Charles Kettering, director of General Motors Research, to write a 1929 magazine article called "Keep the Consumer Dissatisfied." He wasn't suggesting that manufacturers produce shoddy products. Along with many of his corporate cohorts, he was defining a strategic shift for American industry—from fulfilling basic human needs to creating new ones.

In a 1927 interview with the magazine *Nation's Business,* Secretary of Labor James J. Davis provided some numbers to illustrate a problem that the *New York Times* called "need saturation." Davis noted that "the textile mills of this country can produce all the cloth needed in six months' operation each year" and that 14 percent of the American shoe factories could produce a year's supply of footwear. The magazine went on to suggest, "It may be that the world's needs ultimately will be produced by three days' work a week."

Business leaders were less than enthusiastic about the prospect of a society no longer centered on the production of goods. For them, the new "labor-saving" machinery presented not a vision of liberation but a threat to their position at the center of power. John E. Edgerton, president of the National Association of Manufacturers, typified their response when he declared: "I am for everything that will make work happier but against everything that will further subordinate its importance. The emphasis should be put on work—more work and better work." "Nothing," he claimed, "breeds radicalism more than unhappiness unless it is leisure."

By the late 1920s, America's business and political elite had found a way to defuse the dual threat of stagnating economic growth and a radicalized working class in what one industrial consultant called "the gospel of consumption"—the notion that people could be convinced that however much they have, it isn't enough. President Herbert Hoover's 1929 Committee on Recent Economic Changes observed in glowing terms the results: "By advertising and other promotional devices . . . a measurable pull on production has been created which releases capital otherwise tied up." They celebrated the conceptual breakthrough: "Economically we have a boundless field before us; that there are new wants which will make way endlessly for newer wants, as fast as they are satisfied."

Today "work and more work" is the accepted way of doing things. If anything, improvements to the labor-saving machinery since the 1920s have intensified the trend. Machines *can* save labor, but only if they go idle when we possess enough of what they *can* produce. In other words, the machinery offers us an opportunity to work less, an opportunity that as a society we have chosen not to take. Instead, we have allowed the owners of those machines to define their purpose: not reduction of labor, but "higher productivity"—and with it the imperative to consume virtually everything that the machinery can possibly produce.

From the earliest days of the Age of Consumerism there were critics. One of the most influential was Arthur Dahlberg, whose 1932 book *Jobs, Machines, and Capitalism* was well known to policymakers and elected officials in Washington. Dahlberg declared that "failure to shorten the length of the working day . . . is the primary cause of our rationing of opportunity, our excess industrial plant, our enormous wastes of competition, our high pressure advertising, [and] our economic imperialism." Since much of what industry produced was no longer aimed at satisfying human physical needs, a four-hour workday, he claimed, was necessary to prevent society from becoming disastrously materialistic. "By not shortening the working day when all the wood is in," he suggested, the profit motive becomes "both the creator and satisfier of spiritual needs." For when the profit motive can turn nowhere else, "it wraps our soap in pretty boxes and tries to convince us that that is solace to our souls."

There was, for a time, a visionary alternative. In 1930 Kellogg Company, the world's leading producer of ready-to-eat cereal, announced that all of its nearly fifteen hundred workers would move from an eight-hour to a six-hour workday. Company president Lewis Brown and owner W. K. Kellogg noted that if the company ran "four six-hour shifts . . . instead of three eight-hour shifts, this will give work and paychecks to the heads of three hundred more families in Battle Creek."

This was welcome news to workers at a time when the country was rapidly descending into the Great Depression. But as Benjamin Hunnicutt explains in his book *Kellogg's Six-Hour Day*, Brown and Kellogg wanted to do more than save jobs. They hoped to show that the "free exchange of goods, services, and labor in the free market would not have to mean mindless consumerism or eternal exploitation of people and natural resources." Instead "workers would be liberated by increasingly higher wages and shorter hours for the final freedom promised by the Declaration of Independence—the pursuit of happiness."

To be sure, Kellogg did not intend to stop making a profit. But the company leaders argued that men and women would work more efficiently on shorter shifts, and with more people employed, the overall purchasing power of the community would increase, thus allowing for more purchases of goods, including cereals.

A shorter workday did entail a cut in overall pay for workers. But Kellogg raised the hourly rate to partially offset the loss and provided for production bonuses to encourage people to work hard. The company eliminated time off for lunch, assuming that workers would rather work their shorter shift and leave as soon as possible. In a "personal letter" to employees, Brown pointed to the "mental income" of "the enjoyment of the surroundings of your home, the place you work, your neighbors, the other pleasures you have [that are] harder to translate into dollars and cents." Greater leisure, he hoped, would lead to "higher standards in school and civic . . . life" that would benefit the company by allowing it to "draw its workers from a community where good homes predominate."

It was an attractive vision, and it worked. Not only did Kellogg prosper, but journalists from magazines such as *Forbes* and *BusinessWeek* reported that the great majority of company employees embraced the shorter workday. One reporter described "a lot of gardening and community beautification, athletics and hobbies . . . libraries well patronized and the mental background of these fortunate workers . . . becoming richer."

A U.S. Department of Labor survey taken at the time, as well as interviews Hunnicutt conducted with former workers, confirm this picture. The government interviewers noted that "little dissatisfaction with lower earnings resulting from the decrease in hours was expressed, although in the majority of cases very real decreases had resulted." One man spoke of "more time at home with the family." Another remembered: "I could go home and have time to work in my garden." A woman noted that the six-hour shift allowed her husband to "be with 4 boys at ages it was important."

Those extra hours away from work also enabled some people to accomplish things that they might never have been able to do otherwise. Hunnicutt describes how at the end of her interview an eighty-year-old woman began talking about ping-pong. "We'd get together. We had a ping-pong table and all my relatives would come for dinner and things and we'd all play ping-pong by the hour." Eventually she went on to win the state championship.

Many women used the extra time for housework. But even then, they often chose work that drew in the entire family, such as canning. One recalled how canning food at home became "a family project" that "we all enjoyed," including her sons, who "opened up to talk freely." As Hunnicutt puts it, canning became the "medium for something more important than preserving food. Stories, jokes, teasing, quarreling, practical instruction, songs, griefs, and problems were shared. The modern discipline of alienated work was left behind for an older . . . more convivial kind of working together."

This was the stuff of a human ecology in which thousands of small, almost invisible, interactions between family members, friends, and neighbors create an intricate structure that supports social life in much the same way as topsoil supports our biological existence. When we allow either one to become impoverished, whether out of greed or intemperance, we put our long-term survival at risk.

Our modern predicament is a case in point. By 2005 per capita household spending (in inflation-adjusted dollars) was twelve times what it had been in 1929, while per capita spending for durable goods—the big stuff such as cars and appliances—was thirty-two times higher. Meanwhile, by 2000 the average married couple with children was working almost five hundred hours a year more than in 1979. And according to reports by the Federal Reserve Bank in 2004 and 2005, over 40 percent of American families spend more than they earn. The average household carries $18,654 in debt, not including home-mortgage debt, and the ratio of household debt to income is at record levels, having roughly doubled over the last two decades. We are quite literally working ourselves into a frenzy just so we can consume all that our machines can produce.

Yet we could work and spend a lot less and still live quite comfortably. By 1991 the amount of goods and services produced for each hour of labor was double what it had been in 1948. By 2006 that figure had risen another 30 percent. In other words, if as a society we made a collective decision to get by on the amount we produced and consumed seventeen years ago, we could cut back from the standard forty-hour week to

5.3 hours per day—or 2.7 hours if we were willing to return to the 1948 level. We were already the richest country on the planet in 1948 and most of the world has not yet caught up to where we were then.

Rather than realizing the enriched social life that Kellogg's vision offered us, we have impoverished our human communities with a form of materialism that leaves us in relative isolation from family, friends, and neighbors. We simply don't have time for them. Unlike our great-grandparents who passed the time, we spend it. An outside observer might conclude that we are in the grip of some strange curse, like a modern-day King Midas whose touch turns everything into a product built around a microchip.

Of course not everybody has been able to take part in the buying spree on equal terms. Millions of Americans work long hours at poverty wages while many others can find no work at all. However, as advertisers well know, poverty does not render one immune to the gospel of consumption.

Meanwhile, the influence of the gospel has spread far beyond the land of its origin. Most of the clothes, video players, furniture, toys, and other goods Americans buy today are made in distant countries, often by underpaid people working in sweatshop conditions. The raw material for many of those products comes from clearcutting or strip mining or other disastrous means of extraction. Here at home, business activity is centered on designing those products, financing their manufacture, marketing them—and counting the profits.

Kellogg's vision, despite its popularity with his employees, had little support among his fellow business leaders. But Dahlberg's book had a major influence on Senator (and future Supreme Court justice) Hugo Black who, in 1933, introduced legislation requiring a thirty-hour workweek. Although Roosevelt at first appeared to support Black's bill, he soon sided with the majority of businessmen who opposed it. Instead, Roosevelt went on to launch a series of policy initiatives that led to the forty-hour standard that we more or less observe today.

By the time the Black bill came before Congress, the prophets of the gospel of consumption had been developing their tactics and techniques for at least a decade. However, as the Great Depression deepened, the public mood was uncertain, at best, about the proper role of the large corporation. Labor unions were gaining in both public support and legal legitimacy, and the Roosevelt administration, under its New Deal program, was implementing government regulation of industry on an unprecedented scale. Many corporate leaders saw the New Deal as a serious threat. James A. Emery, general counsel for the National Association of Manufacturers (NAM), issued a "call to arms" against the "shackles of irrational regulation" and the "back-breaking burdens of taxation," characterizing the New Deal doctrines as "alien invaders of our national thought."

In response, the industrial elite represented by NAM, including General Motors, the big steel companies, General Foods, DuPont, and others, decided to create their own propaganda. An internal NAM memo called for "re-selling all of the individual Joe Doakes on the advantages and benefits he enjoys under a competitive economy." NAM launched a massive public relations campaign it called the "American Way." As the minutes of a NAM meeting described it, the purpose of the campaign was to link "free enterprise in the public consciousness with free speech, free press and free religion as integral parts of democracy."

Consumption was not only the linchpin of the campaign; it was also recast in political terms. A campaign booklet put out by the J. Walter Thompson advertising agency told readers that under "private capitalism, the *Consumer*, the *Citizen* is boss," and "he doesn't have to wait for election day to vote or for the Court to convene before handing down his verdict. The consumer 'votes' each time he buys one article and rejects another."

According to Edward Bernays, one of the founders of the field of public relations and a principal architect of the American Way, the choices available in the polling booth are akin to those at the department store; both should consist of a limited set of offerings that are carefully determined by what Bernays called an "invisible government" of public-relations experts and advertisers working on behalf of business leaders. Bernays claimed that in a "democratic society" we are and should be "governed, our minds . . . molded, our tastes formed, our ideas suggested, largely by men we have never heard of."

NAM formed a national network of groups to ensure that the booklet from J. Walter Thompson and similar material appeared in libraries and school curricula across the country. The campaign also placed favorable articles in newspapers (often citing "independent" scholars who were paid secretly) and created popular magazines and film shorts directed to children and adults with such titles as "Building Better Americans," "The Business of America's People Is Selling," and "America Marching On."

Perhaps the biggest public relations success for the American Way campaign was the 1939 New York World's Fair. The fair's director of public relations called it "the greatest public relations program in industrial history," one that would battle what he called the "New Deal propaganda." The fair's motto was "Building the World of Tomorrow," and it was indeed a forum in which American corporations literally modeled the future they were determined to create. The most famous of the exhibits was General Motors' 35,000-square-foot Futurama, where visitors toured Democracity, a metropolis of multilane highways that took its citizens from their countryside homes to their jobs in the skyscraper-packed central city.

For all of its intensity and spectacle, the campaign for the American Way did not create immediate, widespread, enthusiastic support for American corporations or the corporate vision of the future. But it did lay the ideological groundwork for changes that came after the Second World War, changes that established what is still commonly called our post-war society.

The war had put people back to work in numbers that the New Deal had never approached, and there was considerable fear that unemployment would return when the war ended. Kellogg workers had been working forty-eight-hour weeks during the war and the majority of them were ready to return to a six-hour day and thirty-hour week. Most of them were able to do so, for a while. But W. K. Kellogg and Lewis Brown had turned the company over to new managers in 1937.

The new managers saw only costs and no benefits to the six-hour day, and almost immediately after the end of the war they began a campaign to undermine shorter hours. Management offered workers a tempting set of financial incentives if they would accept an eight-hour day. Yet in a vote taken in 1946, 77 percent of the men and 87 percent of the women wanted to return to a thirty-hour week rather than a forty-hour one. In making that choice, they also chose a fairly dramatic drop in earnings from artificially high wartime levels.

The company responded with a strategy of attrition, offering special deals on a department-by-department basis where eight hours had pockets of support, typically among highly skilled male workers. In the culture of a post-war, post-Depression U.S., that strategy was largely successful. But not everyone went along. Within Kellogg there was a substantial, albeit slowly dwindling group of people Hunnicutt calls the "mavericks," who resisted longer work hours. They clustered in a few departments that had managed to preserve the six-hour day until the company eliminated it once and for all in 1985.

The mavericks rejected the claims made by the company, the union, and many of their co-workers that the extra money they could earn on an eight-hour shift was worth it. Despite the enormous difference in societal wealth between the 1930s and the 1980s, the language the mavericks used to explain their preference for a six-hour workday was almost identical to that used by Kellogg workers fifty years earlier. One woman, worried about the long hours worked by her son, said, "He has no time to live, to visit and spend time with his family, and to do the other things he really loves to do."

Several people commented on the link between longer work hours and consumerism. One man said, "I was getting along real good, so there was no use in me working any more time than I had to." He added, "Everybody thought they were going to get rich when they got that eight-hour deal and it really didn't make a big difference. . . . Some went out and bought automobiles right quick and they didn't gain much on that because the car took the extra money they had."

The mavericks, well aware that longer work hours meant fewer jobs, called those who wanted eight-hour shifts plus overtime "work hogs." "Kellogg's was laying off people," one woman commented, "while some of the men were working really fantastic amounts of overtime—that's just not fair." Another quoted the historian Arnold Toynbee, who said, "We will either share the work, or take care of people who don't have work."

People in the Depression-wracked 1930s, with what seems to us today to be a very low level of material goods, readily chose fewer work hours for the same reasons as some of their children and grandchildren did in the 1980s: to have more time for themselves and their families. We could, as a society, make a similar choice today.

But we cannot do it as individuals. The mavericks at Kellogg held out against company and social pressure for years, but in the end the marketplace didn't offer them a choice to work less and consume less. The reason is simple: that choice is at odds with the foundations of the marketplace itself—at least as it is currently constructed. The men and women who masterminded the creation of the consumerist society understood that theirs was a political undertaking, and it will take a powerful political movement to change course today.

Bernays's version of a "democratic society," in which political decisions are marketed to consumers, has many modern proponents. Consider a comment by Andrew Card, George W. Bush's former chief of staff. When asked why the administration waited several months before making its case for war against Iraq, Card replied, "You don't roll out a new product in August." And in 2004, one of the leading legal theorists in the United States, federal judge Richard Posner, declared that "representative democracy . . . involves a division between rulers and ruled," with the former being "a governing class," and the rest of us exercising a form of "consumer sovereignty" in the political sphere with "the power not to buy a particular product, a power to choose though not to create."

Sometimes an even more blatant antidemocratic stance appears in the working papers of elite think tanks. One such example is the prominent Harvard political scientist Samuel Huntington's 1975 contribution to a Trilateral Commission report on "The Crisis of Democracy." Huntington warns against an "excess of democracy," declaring that "a democratic political system usually requires some measure of apathy and noninvolvement on the part of some individuals and groups." Huntington notes that "marginal social groups, as in the case of the blacks, are now becoming full participants in the political system" and thus present the "danger of overloading the political system" and undermining its authority.

According to this elite view, the people are too unstable and ignorant for self-rule. "Commoners," who are viewed as factors of production at work and as consumers at home, must adhere to their proper roles in order to maintain social stability. Posner, for example, disparaged a proposal for a national day of deliberation as "a small but not trivial reduction in the amount of productive work." Thus he appears to be an ideological descendant of the business leader who warned that relaxing the imperative for "more work and better work" breeds "radicalism."

As far back as 1835, Boston workingmen striking for shorter hours declared that they needed time away from work to be good citizens: "We have rights, and we have duties to perform as American citizens and members of society." As those workers well understood, any meaningful democracy requires citizens who are empowered to create and re-create their government, rather than a mass of marginalized voters who merely choose from what is offered by an "invisible" government. Citizenship requires a commitment of time and attention, a commitment people cannot make if they are lost to themselves in an ever-accelerating cycle of work and consumption.

We can break that cycle by turning off our machines when they have created enough of what we need. Doing so will give us an opportunity to re-create the kind of healthy communities that were beginning to emerge with Kellogg's six-hour day, communities in which human welfare is the overriding concern rather than subservience to machines and those who own them. We can create a society where people have time to play together as well as work together, time to act politically in their common interests, and time even to argue over what those common interests might be. That fertile mix of human relationships is necessary for healthy human societies, which in turn are necessary for sustaining a healthy planet.

If we want to save the Earth, we must also save ourselves from ourselves. We can start by sharing the work *and* the wealth. We may just find that there is plenty of both to go around.

(2008)

DERRICK JENSEN

FORGET SHORTER SHOWERS

Why personal change does not equal political change

WOULD ANY SANE PERSON think dumpster diving would have stopped Hitler, or that composting would have ended slavery or brought about the eight-hour workday, or that chopping wood and carrying water would have gotten people out of Tsarist prisons, or that dancing naked around a fire would have helped put in place the Voting Rights Act of 1957 or the Civil Rights Act of 1964? Then why now, with all the world at stake, do so many people retreat into these entirely personal "solutions"?

Part of the problem is that we've been victims of a campaign of systematic misdirection. Consumer culture and the capitalist mindset have taught us to substitute acts of personal consumption (or enlightenment) for organized political resistance. *An Inconvenient Truth* helped raise consciousness about global warming. But did you notice that all of the solutions presented had to do with personal consumption—changing light bulbs, inflating tires, driving half as much—and had nothing to do with shifting power away from corporations, or

stopping the growth economy that is destroying the planet?
Even if every person in the United States did everything the
movie suggested, U.S. carbon emissions would fall by only
22 percent. Scientific consensus is that emissions must be
reduced by at least 75 percent worldwide.

Or let's talk water. We so often hear that the world is running out of water. People are dying from lack of water. Rivers
are dewatered from lack of water. Because of this we need
to take shorter showers. See the disconnect? *Because I take
showers, I'm responsible for drawing down aquifers?* Well, no.
More than 90 percent of the water used by humans is used
by agriculture and industry. The remaining 10 percent is split
between municipalities and actual living breathing individual
humans. Collectively, municipal golf courses use as much water as municipal human beings. People (both human people
and fish people) aren't dying because the world is running out
of water. They're dying because the water is being stolen.

Or let's talk energy. Kirkpatrick Sale summarized it well:
"For the past 15 years the story has been the same every year:
individual consumption—residential, by private car, and so
on—is never more than about a quarter of all consumption;
the vast majority is commercial, industrial, corporate, by
agribusiness and government [he forgot military]. So, even
if we all took up cycling and wood stoves it would have a
negligible impact on energy use, global warming and atmospheric pollution."

Or let's talk waste. In 2005, per-capita municipal waste
production (basically everything that's put out at the curb)
in the U.S. was about 1,660 pounds. Let's say you're a die-
hard simple-living activist, and you reduce this to zero. You
recycle everything. You bring cloth bags shopping. You fix
your toaster. Your toes poke out of old tennis shoes. You're
not done yet, though. Since municipal waste includes not just

residential waste, but also waste from government offices and businesses, you march to those offices, waste reduction pamphlets in hand, and convince them to cut down on their waste enough to eliminate your share of it. Uh, I've got some bad news. Municipal waste accounts for only 3 percent of total waste production in the United States.

I want to be clear. I'm not saying we shouldn't live simply. I live reasonably simply myself, but I don't pretend that not buying much (or not driving much, or not having kids) is a powerful political act, or that it's deeply revolutionary. It's not. Personal change doesn't equal social change.

So how, then, and especially with all the world at stake, have we come to accept these utterly insufficient responses? I think part of it is that we're in a double bind. A double bind is where you're given multiple options, but no matter what option you choose, you lose, and withdrawal is not an option. At this point, it should be pretty easy to recognize that every action involving the industrial economy is destructive (and we shouldn't pretend that solar photovoltaics, for example, exempt us from this: they still require mining and transportation infrastructures at every point in the production processes; the same can be said for every other so-called green technology). So if we choose option one—if we avidly participate in the industrial economy—we may in the short term think we win because we may accumulate wealth, the marker of "success" in this culture. But we lose, because in doing so we give up our empathy, our animal humanity. And we really lose because industrial civilization is killing the planet, which means everyone loses. If we choose the "alternative" option of living more simply, thus causing less harm, but still not stopping the industrial economy from killing the planet, we may in the short term think we win because we get to feel pure, and we didn't even have to give up all of our empathy (just enough to justify not stopping the horrors), but once again we really lose because industrial civilization is still killing the planet, which means everyone still loses. The third option, acting decisively to stop the industrial economy, is very scary for a number of reasons, including but not restricted to the fact that we'd lose some of the luxuries (like electricity) to which we've grown accustomed, and the fact that those in power might try to kill us if we seriously impede their ability to exploit the world—none of which alters the fact that it's a better option than a dead planet. Any option is a better option than a dead planet.

Besides being ineffective at causing the sorts of changes necessary to stop this culture from killing the planet, there are at least four other problems with perceiving simple living as a political act (as opposed to living simply because that's what you want to do). The first is that it's predicated on the flawed notion that humans inevitably harm their landbase. Simple living as a political act consists solely of harm reduction, ignoring the fact that humans can help the Earth as well as harm it. We can rehabilitate streams, we can get rid of noxious invasives, we can remove dams, we can disrupt a political system tilted toward the rich as well as an extractive economic system, we can destroy the industrial economy that is destroying the real, physical world.

The second problem—and this is another big one—is that it incorrectly assigns blame to the individual (and most especially to individuals who are particularly powerless) instead of to those who actually wield power in this system and to the system itself. Kirkpatrick Sale again: "The whole individualist what-you-can-do-to-save-the-earth guilt trip is a myth. We, as individuals, are not creating the crises, and we can't solve them."

The third problem is that it accepts capitalism's redefinition of us from citizens to consumers. By accepting this redefinition, we reduce our potential forms of resistance to consuming and not consuming. Citizens have a much wider range of available resistance tactics, including voting, not voting, running for office, pamphleting, boycotting, organizing, lobbying, protesting, and, when a government becomes destructive of life, liberty, and the pursuit of happiness, we have the right to alter or abolish it.

The fourth problem is that the endpoint of the logic behind simple living as a political act is suicide. If every act within an industrial economy is destructive, and if we want to stop this destruction, and if we are unwilling (or unable) to question (much less destroy) the intellectual, moral, economic, and physical infrastructures that cause every act within an industrial economy to be destructive, then we can easily come to believe that we will cause the least destruction possible if we are dead.

The good news is that there are other options. We can follow the examples of brave activists who lived through the difficult times I mentioned—Nazi Germany, Tsarist Russia, antebellum United States—who did far more than manifest a form of moral purity; they actively opposed the injustices that surrounded them. We can follow the example of those who remembered that the role of an activist is not to navigate systems of oppressive power with as much integrity as possible, but rather to confront and take down those systems.

(2009)

JANISSE RAY

ALTAR CALL FOR TRUE BELIEVERS

Are we being change, or are we just talking about change?

IF I EVER PREACHED to the choir, this luncheon was it. The sixty people in the room were professed environmentalists, all of them on the advisory council of an earth center at a college that advertises itself, rightfully, as strongly committed to environmental responsibility. Seated to my right was a friendly but road-weary woman who had arrived minutes before from Chicago. She had rented a car at the airport and driven straight here.

"When will you return home?" I asked.

"I'll go back this afternoon," she said.

My white cloth napkin lay folded in my lap. Two silver forks waited to the left of my plate. In minutes I would rise to speak at a meal for which and only for which one woman had flown from Illinois to North Carolina. In fact, I was speaking about the climate crisis. Could anything I said be worth those 750 pounds of carbon dioxide blasted into the atmosphere? Fifty-nine other people had journeyed here by various conveyances. Surely I was in part responsible.

That afternoon, on a panel at the same college, I was asked to discuss "walking the talk." As invariably happens in the company in which I often find myself, someone referred to the audience as "the choir" and to us panelists as "ministers"—"What can we do to quit just preaching to the choir?"

By "choir" I assume the person meant the *already converted*, the *dedicated*, the *environmentalists*, which implies that somewhere out in the big world there are people who have not yet seen the light, or have seen the light but have not accepted it as their savior, and that our job might more necessarily be to bring those people into the fold. Another person raised her hand and talked about how the uneducated firefighters at the station where she volunteers drive F-150s and employ chemicals to green their lawns. "Where are *those* people today?" she asked.

As missionaries, the choir member implied, we are failing.

I looked around the room, trying to find the so-called choir. I have been trying to find the choir for a long time, and even more importantly, *have been trying to join the choir*. From where I stand, even the choir seems to be failing. Or as my friend Dave Brown put it, the choir may be much smaller than we thought.

Many years ago a man I revere, a forest ecologist who has done more than anybody I know to promote his home ecosystem, revealed to me that he shoots hawks. He and his wife love the birds that flock to their butterfly gardens; they love to watch them through a floor-to-ceiling bird window. Yet my mentor loves the colorful songbirds more than he loves the raptors they attract, and in this conflict of interest the ecologist kills hawks.

This private confession of a forest ecologist caused a great turmoil in me. Whitman, of course, said, "Do I contradict myself? Very well, then, I contradict myself." But I'm a purist. I like black and white. I like hawks.

I fear what this choir—the one I attempt to sing in and occasionally preach to—actually looks like.

At risk of appearing a fraud, I want to admit my own culpability right up front. I live in a comfortable house in the small city of Brattleboro, Vermont. My husband and I cut trees to heat our home, and some of them are alive when we fell them. On the coldest days we turn to fossil fuels to keep the house above sixty degrees. We drive vehicles that consume fossil fuels, and we have raised a son who also now drives a gasoline-powered vehicle. We even own a motorboat. Our home uses electricity that, in part, is produced by the Vermont Yankee nuclear plant. I fly regularly. Never having been to Europe, I'd like to take my family there someday, and chances are we'll fly.

A portion of the food we buy is trucked or flown to us from a shocking distance. We have three dogs, demanding their own portions of the Earth's resources. Somehow my desk holder is always filled with disposable pens. I shave my legs, and I don't do it with a straight edge. I've purchased clothing at times that was surely made in sweatshops. So, perfect I am not. In fact, my part in the destruction of nature is both serious and shameful.

Yet many times a day, I move ever toward a more sustainable life, learning to weigh the implications of my actions. To measure sustainability, I often refer to Jim Merkel's definition, which is human consumption based on biospheric production or, using the Earth's resources at a rate *slower* than they regenerate. Step by step I creep toward a life that is easier on the planet, eating locally as much as possible, buying secondhand goods, using manual technology instead of electric. For over a year my husband and I saved to buy a hybrid car before purchasing a used one at list price from a friend. A state grant allowed us to exchange every incandescent bulb in our home for a compact fluorescent. Each spring our vegetable garden expands.

These conversions toward sustainability may be easier for me than for some. I was raised very poor—on a junkyard, in fact. I learned almost from infancy to recycle, to make do or do without, to keep needs separate from desires, to waste not. Living within our means taught me to live within the Earth's means. Growing up in a fanatically religious family, too, I learned early that "putting your money where your mouth is" was more than an adage. My family practiced what my father preached.

Still, I am far from saved. My footprint is surely too large for me to enter the kingdom of sustainability heaven. If sustainable living is a continuum, from excessive waste to zero waste, then I too am not where I want to be on it.

However, I gaze out across the continuum and see people—environmentalists!—much farther behind than I expect.

A few people I know who consider themselves environmentalists have purchased new cars recently, ones that run on internal-combustion engines and get less than thirty miles to the gallon. One friend, a global-warming scientist, told me he decided not to buy a hybrid "until the kinks get worked out."

Three other environmentalist friends have built new homes. Full of love and admiration for my friends, I have enjoyed these beautiful homes, all artfully designed, comfortable, well heated, well lit, and *more than 2,500 square feet in size*. All of the houses are connected to the power grid, although one also has solar panels. Another was described to me by my friend, the owner, as "sustainable," by which she meant that some passive solar techniques were employed in its construction and that natural stone was used for the mammoth fireplace. That particular home has a pool and a hot tub.

I watched another friend buy a pint of blueberries from a farmstand and accept a plastic bag offered by the cashier. The minute we got to the car, he removed the blueberries from the bag and we started to eat them. I was brought face to face with a plastic bag whose lifespan was less than five minutes (but whose slow death in a landfill may take more than a thousand years).

Every day, in thousands of actions large and small, we who profess to love the Earth are making decisions that destroy it. Some of these choices are unavoidable, to be sure. But in many cases we could easily choose less harmful options and not suffer measurably, if at all.

Perhaps the hardest thing for me in life is contradiction. There is an ancient enmity between deed and creed, it seems. Knowing the complexity of the human psyche, my own included, I never expect the two to align perfectly. Nor are contradictions easy to recognize in ourselves. However, when words and actions are obviously incongruous, I start to feel crazy, and in the face of new and startling evidence of environmental catastrophe, the contradictions are almost too much to bear.

A global-warming speaker is invited to a village ten miles from Brattleboro to speak. She accepts. There is no effort made to organize a carpool or a bus, and as might be expected, most of the people in the audience, including myself, have motored from town. Or, eighteen hundred land-trust advocates gather in Nashville. I am among them, grimly imagining the jet fuel, gasoline, and oil burned to get eighteen hundred people to a single location.

Some of the contradictions are less dramatic. Last Thanksgiving we ordered a locally grown, organic turkey. When I called, the farmer said that I would need to pick up the turkey on the Sunday prior to Thanksgiving at her farm, located thirty miles away.

"Is there no other way to get it?" I asked. "Do you not deliver to town?"

"The only way we distribute is at the farm."

"I'm very worried about climate change," I said. "Could I have someone else from town pick up my turkey? I'll send a check."

"Listen," she said. "I have ninety turkeys to distribute. I don't have time to find someone who will bring your turkey to you."

"Not necessarily to my door," I said. "I could meet the person in town. If you give me a few numbers, I'll call around and find someone."

"Sorry," she said, annoyed. "I can't give out the names of my customers."

There I was, caught between eating locally and driving sixty miles to pick up a turkey.

And that's the conundrum we all should be facing. Every day we should be weighing even the minutest decision and asking ourselves, Which action causes the least harm? Should I travel these miles? Will my gains in knowledge and inspiration offset my damage to the planet?

In the case of the turkey, I found two other families who'd ordered birds and we rode together to the farm. In the end, the benefits of that particular Thanksgiving fowl still outweighed the costs associated with the mass-produced, store-bought option, but even my share of the miles traveled to fetch it left a bitter taste in my mouth.

We choir members are well educated. We've read *Field Notes from a Catastrophe* and *The Long Emergency* and *The Omni-*

vore's Dilemma. But are we committed enough to really make change? Are we part of being change, or are we just talking about change? Do we consider every decision we make? Do we analyze our own impact and work to decrease it, day by day? Do we continually strive to get by with less?

Or are we, too, alongside the unenlightened multitudes, living in denial, turning our heads from the true consequences of our actions? Are we still living safely, properly? Are we unwilling to give up our memberships? Are we unwilling to look different, to act different, to stand behind our beliefs even if we might be considered eccentric or even losers by the dominant culture? Are we granting ourselves exemptions? Do we justify harmful actions because they're done on behalf of the Earth? Or worse, do we justify them because we think we're already doing enough?

And, having been taught so well to act—to be activists— are we able to see that the best decisions may not look like action? That the right action (as with the Chicagoan) may be staying closer to home?

Many times I have attended some gathering or other to speak about environmental issues, and when the final word has been delivered, the final question debated, refreshments are served on plastic plates and in plastic cups. I prepare my remarks.

I take a deep breath, step in front of the crowd. I rant, I rave, I weep and open my heart. I preach fire and brimstone, and the punch is served in plastic cups. I cannot tell you the horrible feeling that envelops me.

Now, when invited somewhere to speak, I send a sheet ahead of time asking organizers for an environment-friendly event: paper instead of plastics; no Styrofoam; if possible, real flatware and dinnerware; at least biodegradable flatware; recycled paper in fliers and press releases; services provided by local businesses; locally grown and organic food preferred for meals or receptions; receptacles for recycling; carpooling encouraged. These guidelines, with many more that you or I have yet to imagine, are ones that we need to employ every hour of every day. We have to believe with our bodies what we know in our minds to be true. We have to accept the solutions to our environmental problems as personal and start applying them personally, and then all around us.

Given that our government won't ratify the Kyoto Protocol or take steps to limit production of carbon and other greenhouse gases, we choir members have to sign the Kyoto treaty individually, or take a pledge to reduce our personal emissions 30 percent in the next two years and 80 percent by 2050. We also have to keep applying pressure to government, and holding our elected officials accountable. If we're not doing it, who is?

Living a lie destroys the spirit. It is a kind of mental illness, a schizophrenia. It also undermines our credibility. That's why *An Inconvenient Truth* disappointed me. The night the film premiered in Brattleboro, my husband and I bicycled to the theater and waited in line for tickets. Afterward, we were uplifted: we knew millions of people would watch the movie and would change. I remain grateful for the film and the effect it's having, but what I remember most now are its contradictions. In scene after scene, Al Gore gobbles up fossil fuels: he's behind the wheel of an SUV, he's going through customs, he's on a plane, he's being driven through a city. Even when demonstrating a graph about rising temperatures, Mr. Gore doesn't climb a ladder affixed to the wall. No, he mounts a hydraulic lift.

I have been accused of being judgmental. *Lean in instead of leaning out*, I've been told. *Judge not that ye be not judged.* But I wonder if judgment is really a bad habit—or if the social taboo against passing judgment simply allows us to feel safer in our own hypocrisy.

Whether we be heads of state or directors of organizations or worker bees or armchair cheerleaders, we in the choir are leaders and role models. We, of all people, have to show that life can be lived differently, and that the reimagined life can be beautiful, functional, and overflowing with rewards none of us expected.

So the question becomes: what *should* the choir look like? And: what do I have to do to belong?

We can look to Susana Lein for part of the answer. Lein runs Salamander Springs Farm near Berea, Kentucky. She spent the better part of the 1980s as a landscape architect in the Boston area, then seven years living in her husband's native Guatemala, learning to live simply, making do. When her marriage ended, she returned to the United States, bought ninety-eight acres with friends, and began to live on the land in a tent. She farms six acres without tillage or chemicals of any kind. A designer and alternative builder, she is also a person determined to live within her means and the means of the Earth. She built a rough house by raiding dumpsters for building supplies and trading labor with friends. She uses a composting toilet, a spring for water, solar energy.

I heard Lein speak at a Northeast Organic Farming Association conference. What attracted me to her talk was its title: "Creating a Farm and Homestead on Marginal Land (While Penniless)." Humble and unassuming, private and down-to-earth, Susana Lein was the most inspiring person I'd seen in a long time. Without a doubt she walks the talk.

We also need to recognize that others in the choir may not look the way we expect them to. My father the junkman belongs in the choir, although he would never call himself an environmentalist. He's never flown in a passenger jet and

rarely travels by car beyond his home county. He lives simply, makes do. That he never went to college, never read Aldo
Leopold, and may not have heard of carrying capacity matters
not. Now is as good a time as any to shed our preconceptions
about what an environmentalist looks like, and to recognize
that the most unlikely people are going to be allies in the
quest for sustainability.

The good news is that I'm starting to see more determination and more personal accountability. Recently I spoke to environmental educators in North Carolina during an eco-picnic
in a longleaf pine grove on Fort Bragg. The day was sunny and
gorgeous. Lois Nixon, who organized the event, made sure
that picnic lunches were served in reusable cooler bags, that
napkins were cotton washcloths, and that most of the lunch
was local and organic. She distributed compact fluorescent
bulbs (donated to the group) to offset some of the carbon
generated by travel.

A Covington, Georgia, Montessori school sponsored a
reception after a reading I gave at the local public library.
The hors d'oeuvres were bowls of cherry tomatoes and carrot
sticks, grown by local gardeners—no brownies from a box, no
cheese sticks. By using porcelain plates and cloth napkins, the
group met its goal of zero waste.

At the Farmers Diner in Vermont, where we ate on my
birthday, there was not a paper towel to be found in the re-
stroom. On the sink sat a basket of white hand-towels and
underneath, a basket for used ones.

Of course, no matter how many paper cups or napkins
I decline, the fact remains that I fly around the country in a
direct negation of my mission. To scale back this personal
gluttony of fossil fuels, I have been accepting fewer invita-
tions, scheduling multiple events in one area, and combining
business with social visits and research. At home, I bike and

walk a lot. *A lot* is not enough, I know. I am working toward leaving home on my bike more often than in my car, until maybe there's no longer any use for the car.

And when my son goes off to college next fall and I can be away from home for longer periods of time, I intend to put a moratorium on air travel. I'll be taking the train and the bus, which means that I'll think long and hard about going to Arizona for a two-day conference when the journey itself is two days each way. I'll miss some of the travel, but I look forward to the unsurpassable joys of staying close to home—and that joy is the key here, because I'm not preaching a life of deprivation. I'm talking about bringing our actions into better alignment with our aspirations for the Earth.

I want to see our communities get more and more localized, with more local food produced and consumed, more local goods bought and sold. I want to see local entrepreneurship and craftsmanship encouraged. I want a renaissance of the hands, so that we use fewer electrical gadgets and motorized tools.

I want to hear of an organization that decides, because of the climate crisis, to cancel its annual conference. I want to see us relying on the mail and conference calls and e-mail for corresponding with distant colleagues, and engaging more deliberately with our neighbors. I want to see us using petroleum as if it were precious, which is to say sparingly and wisely, driving shorter distances and less often; in fact, I want getting in a single-occupancy vehicle to be a last resort.

I want us to get radical. I want us choir members to make even the hardest decisions while holding the Earth in mind.

I want us to raise the bar for ourselves.

(2007)

JAMES HOWARD KUNSTLER

MAKING OTHER ARRANGEMENTS

A wake-up call to a citizenry in the shadow of oil scarcity

As THE AMERICAN PUBLIC continues sleepwalking into a future of energy scarcity, climate change, and geopolitical turmoil, we have also continued dreaming. Our collective dream is one of those super-vivid ones people have just before awakening. It is a particularly American dream on a particularly American theme: how to keep all the cars running by some other means than gasoline. *We'll run them on ethanol! We'll run them on biodiesel, on synthesized coal liquids, on hydrogen, on methane gas, on electricity, on used French-fry oil . . . !*
The dream goes around in fevered circles as each gasoline replacement is examined and found to be inadequate. But the wish to keep the cars going is so powerful that round and round the dream goes. *Ethanol! Biodiesel! Coal liquids . . .*
And a harsh reality indeed awaits us as the full scope of the permanent energy crisis unfolds. According to the U.S. Department of Energy, world oil production peaked in December 2005 at just over 85 million barrels a day. Since then,

it has trended absolutely flat at around 84 million. Yet world oil consumption rose consistently from 77 million barrels a day in 2001 to above 85 million so far this year. A clear picture emerges: demand now exceeds world supply. Or, put another way, oil production has not increased despite the ardent wish that it would by all involved, and despite the overwhelming incentive of prices having nearly quadrupled since 2001.

There is no question that we are in trouble with oil. The natural gas situation is comparably ominous, with some differences in the technical details—and by the way, I am referring here to methane gas (CH_4), the stuff that fuels kitchen stoves and home furnaces, not cars and trucks. Natural gas doesn't deplete slowly like oil, following a predictable bell-curve pattern; it simply stops coming out of the ground when a particular gas well is played out. You also tend to get your gas from the continent you are on. To import natural gas from overseas, it has to be liquefied, loaded in a special kind of expensive-to-build-and-operate tanker, and then offloaded at a specialized marine terminal.

Half the homes in America are heated with gas furnaces and about 16 percent of our electricity is made with it. Industry uses natural gas as the primary ingredient in fertilizer, plastics, ink, glue, paint, laundry detergent, insect repellent, and many other common household necessities. Synthetic rubber and man-made fibers like nylon could not be made without the chemicals derived from natural gas. In North America, natural gas production peaked in 1973. We are drilling as fast as we can to keep the air conditioners and furnaces running.

What's more, the problems of climate change are amplifying, ramifying, and mutually reinforcing the problems associated with rapidly vanishing oil and gas reserves. This was illustrated vividly in 2005, when slightly higher ocean temperatures sent Hurricanes Katrina and Rita slamming into the U.S. Gulf Coast. Almost a year later, roughly 12 percent of oil production and 9.5 percent of natural gas production in the gulf was still out, probably for good. Many of these production platforms may never be rebuilt, because the amounts of oil and gas left beneath them would not justify the cost. If there is $50 million worth of oil down there, why spend $100 million replacing a wrecked platform to get it?

Climate change will also ramify the formidable problems associated with alternative fuels. As I write, the American grain belt is locked in a fierce summer drought. Corn and soybean crops are withering from Minnesota to Illinois; wheat is burning up in the Dakotas and Kansas. Meanwhile, the costs of agricultural "inputs"—from diesel fuel to fertilizers made from natural gas to oil-derived pesticides—have been ramping up steadily since 2003 to the great distress of farmers. Both weather and oil costs are driving our crop yields down, while the industrial mode of farming that has evolved since the Second World War becomes increasingly impractical. We are going to have trouble feeding ourselves in the years ahead, not to mention the many nations who depend for survival on American grain exports. So the idea that we can simply shift millions of acres from food crops to ethanol or biodiesel crops to make fuels for cars represents a staggering misunderstanding of reality.

Still, the widespread wish persists that some combination of alternative fuels will rescue us from this oil and gas predicament and allow us to continue enjoying by some other means what Vice-President Cheney has called the "non-negotiable" American way of life. The truth is that no combination of alternative fuels or systems for using them will allow us to continue running America, or even a substantial fraction of it, the way we have been. We are not going to run Wal-Mart, Walt

Disney World, Monsanto, and the Interstate Highway System on any combination of solar or wind energy, hydrogen, ethanol, tar sands, oil shale, methane hydrates, nuclear power, thermal depolymerization, "zero-point" energy, or anything else you can name. We will desperately use many of these things in many ways, but we are likely to be disappointed in what they can actually do for us.

The key to understanding the challenge we face is admitting that we have to comprehensively make other arrangements for all the normal activities of everyday life. I will return to this theme shortly, but first it is important to try to account for the extraordinary amount of delusional thinking that currently dogs our collective ability to think about these problems.

The widespread wish to just uncouple from oil and gas and plug all our complex systems into other energy sources is an interesting and troubling enough phenomenon in its own right to merit some discussion. Perhaps the leading delusion is the notion that energy and technology are one and the same thing, interchangeable. The popular idea, expressed incessantly in the news media, is that if you run out of energy, you just go out and find some "new technology" to keep things running. We'll learn that this doesn't comport with reality. For example, commercial airplanes are either going to run on cheap liquid hydrocarbon fuels or we're not going to have commercial aviation as we have known it. No other energy source is concentrated enough by weight, affordable enough by volume, and abundant enough in supply to do the necessary work to overcome gravity in a loaded airplane, repeated thousands of times each day by airlines around the world. No other way of delivering that energy source besides refined liquid hydrocarbons will allow that commercial system to operate at the scale we are accustomed to. The only reason this system exists is that until now such fuels have been cheap and abundant. We are not going to replace the existing worldwide fleet of airplanes either, and besides, there is no other type of airplane we have yet devised that can work differently.

There may be other ways of moving things above the ground, for instance balloons, blimps, or zeppelin-type airships. But they will move much more slowly and carry far less cargo and human passengers than the airplanes we've been enjoying for the past sixty years or so. The most likely scenario in the years ahead is that aviation will become an increasingly expensive, elite activity as the oil age dribbles to a close, and then it will not exist at all.

Another major mistake made by those who fail to pay attention is overlooking the unanticipated consequences of new technology, which more often than not add additional layers of problems to existing ones. In the energy sector, one of the most vivid examples is seen in the short history of the world's last truly great oil discovery, the North Sea fields between Norway and the UK. They were found in the '60s, got into production in the late '70s, and were pumping at full blast in the early '90s. Then, around 1999, they peaked and are now in extremely steep decline—up to 50 percent a year in the case of some UK fields. The fact that they were drilled with the latest and best new technology turns out to mean that they were drained with stunning efficiency. "New technology" only hastened Britain's descent into energy poverty. Now, after a twenty-year-long North Sea bonanza in which it enjoyed an orgy of suburbanization, Great Britain is again a net energy importer. Soon the Brits will have no North Sea oil whatsoever and will find themselves below their energy diet of the grim 1950s.

If you really want to understand the U.S. public's penchant for wishful thinking, consider this: We invested most of our late twentieth-century wealth in a living arrangement with no future. American suburbia represents the greatest misallocation of resources in the history of the world. The far-flung housing subdivisions, commercial highway strips, big-box stores, and all the other furnishings and accessories of extreme car dependence will function poorly, if at all, in an oil-scarce future. Period. This dilemma now entails a powerful psychology of previous investment, which is prompting us to defend our misinvestments desperately, or, at least, preventing us from letting go of our assumptions about their future value. Compounding the disaster is the unfortunate fact that the manic construction of ever more futureless suburbs (a.k.a. the "housing bubble") has insidiously replaced manufacturing as the basis of our economy.

Meanwhile, the outsourcing of manufacturing to other nations has spurred the development of a "global economy," which media opinion-leaders such as *New York Times* columnist Tom Friedman (author of *The World Is Flat*) say is a permanent state of affairs that we had better get used to. It is probably more accurate to say that the global economy is a set of transient economic relations that have come about because of two fundamental (and transient) conditions: a half century of relative peace between great powers and a half century of cheap and abundant fossil-fuel energy. These two mutually dependent conditions are now liable to come to an end as the great powers enter a bitter contest over the world's remaining energy resources, and the world is actually apt to become a lot larger and less flat as these economic relations unravel.

This is approximately the state of the nation right now. It is deeply and tragically ironic that the more information that bombards us, the less we seem to understand. There are cable TV news networks and internet news sites beyond counting, yet we are unable to process this deluge of information into a coherent public discussion about the fundamental challenges that our civilization faces—not to mention a sensible agenda for meeting these hardships. Meanwhile, *CBS News* tells millions of viewers that the tar sands of Alberta will solve all our problems, or (two weeks later) that the coal beds under Montana and Wyoming will sustain business as usual, and CNN tells another several million viewers that we can run everything here on ethanol, just like they do in Brazil.

Of course, the single worst impediment to clear thinking among most individuals and organizations in America today is the obsession with keeping the cars running at all costs. Even the environmental community is guilty of this. The esteemed Rocky Mountain Institute ran a project for a decade to design and develop a "hyper-car" capable of getting supernaturally fabulous mileage, in the belief that this would be an ecological benefit. The short-sightedness of this venture? It only promoted the idea that we could continue to be a car-dependent society; the project barely gave nodding recognition to the value of walkable communities and public transit.

The most arrant case of collective cluelessness now on view is our failure to even begin a public discussion about fixing the U.S. passenger railroad system, which has become so decrepit that the Bulgarians would be ashamed of it. It's the one thing we could do right away that would have a substantial impact on our oil use. The infrastructure is still out there, rusting in the rain, waiting to be fixed. The restoration of it would employ hundreds of thousands of Americans at all levels of meaningful work. The fact that we are hardly even talking about it—at any point along the political spectrum, left, right, or center—shows how fundamentally un-serious we are.

This is just not good enough. It is not worthy of our history, our heritage, or the sacrifices that our ancestors made. It is wholly incompatible with anything describable as our collective responsibility to the future.

We have to do better. We have to start right away making those *other arrangements*. We have to begin the transition to some mode of living that will allow us to carry on the project of civilization—and I would argue against the notion advanced by Daniel Quinn and others that civilization itself is our enemy and should not be continued. The agenda for facing our problems squarely can, in fact, be described with some precision. We have to make other arrangements for the basic activities of everyday life.

In general, the circumstances we face with energy and climate change will require us to live much more locally, probably profoundly and intensely so. We have to grow more of our food locally, on a smaller scale than we do now, with fewer artificial "inputs," and probably with more human and animal labor. Farming may come closer to the center of our national economic life than it has been within the memory of anyone alive now. These changes are also likely to revive a menu of social and class conflicts that we also thought we had left behind.

We'll have to reorganize retail trade by rebuilding networks of local economic interdependence. The rise of national chain retail business was an emergent, self-organizing response to the conditions of the late twentieth century. Those conditions are now coming to an end, and the Wal-Mart way of doing business will come to an end with them: the twelve-thousand-mile merchandise supply line to Asian factories; the "warehouse on wheels" made up of thousands of tractor-trailer trucks circulating endlessly between the container-ship ports and the big-box store loading docks. The damage to local economies that the "superstores" leave behind is massive. Not only have they destroyed multilayered local networks for

making and selling things, they destroyed the middle classes
that ran them, and in so doing they destroyed the cultural and
economic fabric of the communities themselves. This is a lot
to overcome. We will have to resume making some things for
ourselves again, and moving them through smaller-scale trade
networks. We may have fewer things to buy overall. The retail
frenzy of recent decades will subside as we struggle to produce things of value and necessarily consume less.

We'll have to make other arrangements for transport-
ing people and goods. Not only do we desperately need to
rebuild the railroad system, but electrifying it—as virtually
all other advanced nations have done—will bring added advantages, since we will be able to run it on a range of things
other than fossil fuels. We should anticipate a revival of
maritime trade on the regional scale, with more use of boats
on rivers, canals, and waterways within the U.S. Many of our
derelict riverfronts and the dying ports of the Great Lakes
may come back to life. If we use trucks at all to move things,
it will be for the very last leg of the journey. The automobile
will be a diminishing presence in our lives and, increasingly,
a luxury that will be resented by those who can no longer
afford to participate in the "happy motoring" utopia. The
interstate highways themselves will require more resources
to maintain than we will be able to muster. For many of us,
the twenty-first century will be less about incessant mobility
than about staying where we are.

We have to inhabit the terrain of North America differently, meaning a return to traditional cities, towns, neighborhoods, and a productive rural landscape that is more than just
strictly scenic or recreational. We will probably see a reversal
of the two-hundred-year-long trend of people moving from the
country and small towns to the big cities. In fact, our big cities
will probably contract substantially, even while they re-densify

at their centers and along their waterfronts. The work of the New Urbanists will be crucial in rebuilding human habitats that have a future. Their achievement so far has been not so much in building "new towns" like Seaside, Florida, or Kentlands, Maryland, but in retrieving a body of knowledge, principle, and methodology for urban design that had been thrown away in our mad effort to build the drive-in suburbs.

It is harder to predict exactly what may happen with education and medicine, except to say that neither can continue to operate as rackets much longer, and that they, like everything else, will have to become smaller in scale and much more local. Our centralized school districts, utterly dependent on the countless daily trips of fleets of yellow buses and oppressive property taxes, have poor prospects for carrying on successfully in an energy-scarce economy. However, we will be a less affluent nation in the post-oil age, and therefore may be hard-pressed to replace them. A new, more locally based education system may arise instead out of home-schooling, as household classes aggregate into new, small, neighborhood schools. College will cease to be a mass-consumer activity, and may only be available to social elites—if it continues to exist at all. Meanwhile, we're in for a pretty stark era of triage as the vast resources of the "medical industry" contract. Even without a global energy crisis bearing down on us, the federal Medicaid and Medicare systems would not survive the future as currently funded.

As a matter of fact, you can state categorically that anything organized on a gigantic scale, whether it is a federal government or the Acme Corporation or the University of Michigan, will probably falter in the energy-scarce future. Therefore, don't pin your hopes on multinational corporations, international NGOs, or any other giant organizations or institutions.

Recent events have caused many of us to fear that we are headed toward a Big Brother kind of governmental tyranny. I think we will be lucky if the federal government can answer the phones, let alone regulate anyone's life, in the post-oil era. As power devolves to the local and regional level, the very purpose of our federal arrangements may come into question. The state governments, with their enormous bureaucracies, may not be better off. Further along in this century, the real political action will likely shift down to the local level, as reconstructed neighborly associations allow people to tackle problems locally with local solutions.

It's a daunting agenda, all right. And some of you are probably wondering how you are supposed to remain hopeful in the face of these enormous tasks. Here's the plain truth, folks: Hope is not a consumer product. You have to generate your own hope. You do that by demonstrating to yourself that you are brave enough to face reality and competent enough to deal with the circumstances that it presents. How we will manage to uphold a decent society in the face of extraordinary change will depend on our creativity, our generosity, and our kindness, and I am confident that we can find these resources within our own hearts, and collectively in our communities.

(2007)

REBECCA SOLNIT

THE SILENCE OF THE LAMBSWOOL CARDIGANS

When Nike was the goddess of victory and shoes still told stories

THERE WAS A TIME not so long ago when everything was recognizable not just as a cup or a coat, but as a cup made by so-and-so out of clay from this bank on the local river or woven by the guy in that house out of wool from the sheep visible on the hills. Then, objects were not purely material, mere commodities, but signs of processes, human and natural, pieces of a story, and the story as well as the stuff sustained life. It's as though every object spoke—some of them must have sung out—in a language everyone could hear, a language that surrounded every object in an aura of its history.

"All commodities are only definite masses of congealed labor-time," said Marx, but who now could dissolve them into their constituent histories of labor and materials, into the stories that made them about the processes of the world, made them part of life even if they were iron or brick, made them

come to life? For decades tales of city kids who didn't know
that milk came from cows have circulated, and the inability of
American teenagers to find Iraq on a map made the rounds
more recently, but who among us can picture precisely where
their sweater or their sugar comes from?

I've been thinking about that because a new shopping
mall has opened up at the eastern foot of the Bay Bridge,
in what was once, according to the newspaper, the biggest
shellmound in northern California (though the town I grew
up in claimed the same distinction for the Miwok mound it
bulldozed without excavation for a shopping center in the
1950s). From the 1870s to the 1920s, this place was Shellmound Park, an amusement park, racetrack, dance hall, and
shooting range, but Prohibition put the pleasure grounds out
of business and the mound was bulldozed for industry. The
remains of seven hundred Ohlone people that an archaeolo-
gist snatched from the construction site in 1924 are still at the
University of California at Berkeley. Meanwhile, the industrialized site hosted paint and pesticide factories that eventually
made it into a wasteland so toxic that those venturing into
it wore moonsuits. It was reclaimed for shopping, and the
cleanup disturbed the Ohlone remains that hadn't already
been bulldozed.

The street that goes out there is still called Shellmound,
but the mall itself hosts all the usual chains that make it
impossible to know if you're in Phoenix or Philadelphia: Victoria's Secret, Williams-Sonoma, Express, all three versions
of the Gap corporation, including Old Navy and Banana
Republic, all laid out on a fake Main Street. Anti-Gap protes-
tors haven't arrived yet, though they are frequent presences
in downtown San Francisco, decrying both the Gap's reli-
ance on sweatshop labor and the clearcutting of old-growth
redwood forests in Mendocino owned by the Gap's CEO (see

Gapsucks.org). But the day the mall opened, activists from the International Indian Treaty Council handed out flyers protesting the desecration of a burial ground. As a substitute for protecting the actual site, the city of Emeryville has offered a website with information about it, as if a place could be relocated to cyberspace. The mall is a distinctly modern site, a space that could be anywhere into which commodities come as if out of nowhere.

In *The Making of the English Working Class*, Engels recounts the crimes behind the production of everyday things—ceramics, ironware, glass, but particularly cotton cloth. He wrote in a time when objects were first becoming silent, and he asked the same thing that the activists from Gapsucks.org do, that we learn the new industrial languages of objects, that we hear the story of children worked into deformity and blindness to make lace, the story of the knifegrinders with a life expectancy of thirty-five years, or nowadays the tales of sweatshop, prison, and child labor. These industrial stories have always been environmental stories too, about factory effluents, cotton chemicals, the timber industry, the petrochemical industry.

Somewhere in the Industrial Age, objects shut up because their creation had become so remote and intricate a process that it was no longer readily knowable. Or they were silenced, because the pleasures of abundance that all the cheap goods offered were only available if those goods were mute about the scarcity and loss that lay behind their creation. Modern advertising—notably for Nike—constitutes an aggressive attempt to displace the meaning of the commodity from its makers, as though you enter into relationship with very tall athletes rather than, say, very thin Vietnamese teenagers when you buy their shoes. It is a stretch to think about Mexican prison labor while contemplating Victoria's

Secret lavender lace boycut panties. The Western Shoshone rancher and land-rights activist Carrie Dann, whose own family graveyard has been flooded by a goldmine pumping out groundwater to get at the gold below, once remarked to me that everyone who buys gold jewelry should have the associated spent ore delivered to their house. At Nevada's mining rates, that would mean a hundred tons of toxic tailings for every one-ounce ring or chain you buy.

The objects are pretty; their stories are hideous, so you get to choose between an alienated and ultimately meaningless world and one that makes terrible demands on you. Most consumers prefer meaningless over complicated, and therefore prefer that objects remain silent. To tell their tales is to be the bearer of bad news—imagine activists as Moses coming down from Sinai but cutting straight to Leviticus, the forty thousand prohibitions: against shrimp (see www.montererybayaquarium.org), against strawberries (methyl bromide, stoop labor), against gold (see www.greatbasinminewatch.org), and on and on. It's what makes radicals and environmentalists seem so grumpy to the would-be consumer.

Maybe the real question is what substances, objects, and products tell stories that don't make people cringe or turn away. For the past half century the process of artmaking has been part of its subject, and this making becomes a symbolic act that attempts to substitute for the silence of all the other objects. But nobody lives by art alone. There's food from the wild, from your own garden, from friends, ancient objects salvaged and flea-marketed, heirlooms and hand-me-downs, local crafts, and a few things still made with the union label, but it's not easy for anyone to stay pure of Payless and Wal-Mart. Good stories too—pricey organic and free-range and shade-grown food that is only available in the hipper stores of the fancier regions—can be a luxury.

Some of the enthusiasm for farmer's markets, which are springing up like mushrooms after rain, is of meeting objects that aren't mute, because you see the people who grew the produce and know the places they come from are not far away. This alternative economy feeds people who want to be nourished by stories and connections, and it's growing. Some farmer's markets are like boutiques with little bunches of peas or raspberries displayed and priced like jewels, but I go to an intensely multiethnic mobscene called Heart of the City Farmer's Market. The food, even some of the organic stuff, is pretty cheap and everyone is present, including the homeless who hang out in that downtown plaza all week anyway, and the locals who use the market to make up for the way supermarkets boycott poor neighborhoods. Seeing the thorn scars on the hands of the rose growers there was as big a step in knowing what constitutes my world as realizing that, in this town where it never snows, our tapwater is all Sierra snowmelt.

What bothers me about the mall is its silence, a silence we mostly live in nowadays; what cheers me are the ways people are learning to read the silent histories of objects and choosing the objects that still sing.

(2003)

CURTIS WHITE

THE BARBARIC HEART

Capitalism and the crisis of nature

THERE IS A FUNDAMENTAL QUESTION that environmentalists are not very good at asking, let alone answering: "Why is
this, the destruction of the natural world, happening?" We or-
dinarily think of environmentalists as people who care about
something called nature or (if they're feeling a little tech-
nocratic, and they usually are) the "environment." They are
concerned, as well they should be, that the lifestyle and economic practices of the industrialized West are not sustainable,
and that nature itself may experience a "system collapse." But
as scientifically sophisticated as environmentalism's thinking
about natural systems can be (especially its ability to measure
change and make predictions about the future based on those
measurements), its conclusions about human involvement in
environmental degradation tend to be very reductive and caus-
al. Environmentalism's analyses tend to be about "sources."
Industrial sources. Nonpoint sources. Urban sources. Smoke-
stack sources. Tailpipe sources. Even natural sources (like the
soon-to-be-released methane from thawing Arctic tundra). But

environmentalism is not very good at asking, "Okay, but *why do we have all of these polluting sources?*"

Because we have not allowed ourselves to ask this question and instead limited ourselves to haplessly trying to turn off sources, our experience has been like Mickey Mouse's in "The Sorcerer's Apprentice": for every berserk broomstick that he hacked in half, two more took its place, implacably carrying buckets of water that, one by one, created a universal deluge. Similarly, for every polluting source that we turn off (or "mitigate," since we can't seem to really turn off anything), another two pop up in its place. For example, at the very moment that we seem to have become serious about reducing our use of petroleum, here comes coal from the ravaged mountaintops of West Virginia and tar sands from Canada, the dirtiest and most destructive energy sources of them all. These rounds of mitigation and evasion are what pass for problem-solving.

Environmentalism is also reluctant to think that its problem may not be of modern origin but something as old as humanity itself. It is committed to a sort of "presentism" in which the culprits are all of recent vintage: Monsanto, Big Oil, developers of suburban sprawl, the modern corporation, you know, the usual suspects. But bad as these things can be (and that's very bad), they are not the unique creators of our problems. And they are not evil, or, as we descendants of the Puritans like to say, "greedy." Simply blaming these entities for traditional moral failings is not adequate to the true situation. At most, by doing so we create an environmentalist melodrama of evildoers opposed by forces of good. (Big Oil versus the Sierra Club.)

After all, isn't it true that what corporations and the individuals who run them try to do is something very human and very familiar? Even admirable? They try to be creative (or innovative, as they like to say). They try to grow. They revel in discovery. They delight in complexity. They have always been major benefactors to education and the arts. (For instance, the merchant capitalists of the Italian Renaissance were also the facilitators of humanism. Where the bankers went, the artists were not far behind.) They try to exercise critical analytic skills in evaluating the world in which they act. They try to help their friends. They try to make the people who are most important to them prosper. They have an astonishing capacity for creative adaptation, even if it is only in the name of preserving their own dominance. In short, they try to win. They try to *thrive*. We should all be so committed to the risk of "living large." The problem is not with these qualities as admirable human qualities. The problem is with *what* exactly it is that they're trying to help thrive.

My claim is that what is behind these activities is not the stereotypical capitalist mentality of cold logic, a lack of normal feelings, and an unbridled appetite for gain. Rather, I see the Barbaric Heart. First, it is important to say that in associating capitalism with the barbaric I am not merely name-calling. This is so because, as I've already suggested, there is something admirable about the astonishingly complex world that capitalism has made. No amount of human or electronic computation can encompass the complexity of the psychological and material world that market capitalism has brought into being. What economists call the "spontaneous order" of the free market stretches if not infinitely then at least unimaginably. At one end there is the miracle of digital technology (are we really supposed to believe that hundreds of hours of music can fit on a device the size of a cigarette pack?). This digital world gets tinier and more powerful every year, and it is substantially the product of capitalist ingenuity. I have to admire it even if, as a person who has spent his life among books, I mostly fear and dislike it. At the other end, there is the continental roaming of shoppers among millions of products that is as vast, in its own way, as the primordial movement of animal herds stretching from horizon to horizon on the Serengeti. Imagine a satellite image illuminating all the activity at shopping malls in the United States on a typical American Saturday afternoon. From a vantage in space, it would look like North America was flowing and glowing with strange life. If you could for a moment exclude the other consequences of this activity (environmental, social, military), you might be tempted to call this vision beautiful. (As in the ambiguous shots of Los Angeles freeways in the movie *Koyaanisqatsi*. The slow, winding flow of headlights comes to look like a natural phenomenon, like watching the northern lights.)

To say that there is something barbaric at work in these accomplishments is to say that there is also something admirable about the Barbaric Heart itself. The Barbaric Heart is not the opposite of the civilized. In fact, the Barbaric Heart *is* civilized, for all the good that does it, and has always happily clad itself in the decorous togas of Rome (as the Ostrogoth King Theodoric did), the pinstripes of Wall Street, and the comfy suburbanity of L. L. Bean. The Barbaric Heart has always wanted to look nice even when it didn't (consider the leisure suit). The barbaric is admirable for its sheer strength, its daring, its energy, and its willingness to take risks. It is taller than we are. It is prouder in the way that a beautiful animal is proud. It is, as Friedrich Nietzsche put it, a "blonde beast." (He mostly thought that was a good thing, or at least better than being a slave.)

Unhappily, beyond its strength and pride and willingness to take on difficult tasks, there is something dangerous to itself and others in the Barbaric Heart. The Barbaric Heart is a great and energetic actor, but it is no better at questioning itself about the meaning of its actions than capitalism is at asking why the unlimited growth of the Gross Domestic Product is good. Capitalism does not ask, "What's the economy for?" Capitalism merely asks it to grow. (It's as if the only alternative to "growth" was "recession," and no one is allowed to be for that.) Nonetheless, questions are in order. The Greek that opens the Gospel according to John reads, "In the beginning was *Logos*." What is the logos (the spirit, the logic) of the Barbaric Heart? In short, in what name does it act?

The natural mode of reasoning for the Barbaric Heart is simple enough to describe. It was the logic not only of the ancient northern hordes, clothed in animal skins, but of the Roman Empire and the Western civilization that followed as well. (That must be our first deconstructive insight: the barbarian is not an "other" to be driven away in the name of civilized virtue.) For the Romans, virtue simply meant success, usually military success. *Valor*. That was the heart of *Romanitas*. For the Roman forces under Scipio Aemilianus at the end of the Third Punic War against Carthage, the routine was well understood: half of the time would be devoted to violence, to killing every human and dog and cat that crossed their path, and half the time would be given to plunder, to the transfer of every valuable material thing back to Rome, especially gold and silver things. Roman violence was above all *orderly*. As a consequence, as Polybius wrote, Rome "billowed in booty."

This is the barbaric calculation: if you can prosper from violence, then you should go ahead and be violent. In short order the Barbaric Heart is led to conclude that in fact *prosperity is dependent on violence*. Therefore, you should be good at violence, for your own sake and the sake of your country. That was Roman *virtu*. Which is a way of saying that the barbaric itself is a form of virtue, especially if you think that winning, surviving, triumphing, and accumulating great wealth are virtues, just as, in order, athletes, Darwinians, military commanders, and capitalists do. Ultimately, these types are all the same. The athlete, the soldier, and the businessman all want to "win," and by whatever means necessary.

Even though the warlike Romans understood every victory as a divine confirmation of their character, virtue *in fact* has very little to do with what the gods think. Virtues are specific to cultures. Barbaric virtues have been challenged by competing ethical organizations like the Stoic virtues of honor, integrity, simplicity, loyalty, and moderation, or the Christian virtues of selflessness, compassion, reverence, humility, faith, and hope. There have been other articulations of virtue as well. Humanism and the Enlightenment advocated the virtues of fraternity and equality before the law. Environmentalism has used all of these articulations at one time or another in its increasingly desperate effort to gain moral traction. What these forms of virtue have in common is that, unlike the Barbaric Heart, they are concerned with articulating a sense of the *whole*.

For the Barbaric Heart, on the other hand, there is nothing that is as real as the self-interested Ego, His Majesty the Sovereign Self. What else could care so blindly about "winning"? But it also feels, at some dark recess of the heart, how pathetically empty this Self is. So the Barbaric Heart grasps at things to fill that emptiness. The histories of ancient warfare always claim that the surest inducement to the warrior to fight was the prospect of being able to cart off the enemy's silver and gold (and women). Plates, jewelry, the objects in temple shrines, precious ornamentation applied to buildings, anything that glittered. With such a prospect at hand, death meant nothing. Through the "right of conquest" (the unwritten law of the ancient world that trumped all written laws) the warrior might at last feel full and real. He might also participate in glory. Why, he could even become virtuous in this way (or, as we still say, a "hero").

Ironically, through this logic the Barbaric Heart also committed not only itself but all of the human and natural world to what the Greeks called tragedy. Tragic fate, for the Greeks, was the understanding that once you put a certain principle in motion, that principle would play itself out. Completely out. And so, as in Aeschylus's tragedies, humans pursue what they perceive to be their own interest only to become "the slave of their own destruction," an apt expression of our current situation on multiple fronts, economic, military, and environmental.

What is tragic is that the bloody end, "the great wound swimming upwards" like a shark (Aeschylus again), is unintended but no less inevitable for that. We don't intend that the pursuit of personal wealth should lead to the bankruptcy of an entire nation, but bankrupt we are. We don't intend that our strategic military actions should lead to an endless and uncontrollable spiraling of violence, but it does. We don't intend that the pursuit of our happiness should lead to the extinction of animals, desertification, drought, famine, mass human migration, violent storms, but all that is presently "swimming upwards" regardless of what we intend.

There are two things that the Barbaric Heart, for all its brutal blond beauty, doesn't get. First, it doesn't look at itself. It is frustrated by questions like "What makes life worth living?" Or it assumes that the answer is obvious: "Winning! Of course." It doesn't even wonder what its relation to other barbarians might be. It doesn't know about solidarity beyond a blind submission to the tribe (the ancient form of that perverse form of loyalty we call patriotism). But it has very little understanding of why self-interest should be sacrificed to a universal good, whatever that is.

Second, the Barbaric Heart doesn't understand, except at the very last moment of anguished recognition, how *suicidal* its activities are. Edward Gibbon's *The Decline and Fall of the Roman Empire* is full of descriptions of the awful moment of animal awareness when the barbarian realizes that he has gone, once again, too far and brought about his own destruction. For example, after the disastrous battle of Hadrianople in 378 AD at which two thirds of the Emperor Valens's Roman army was wiped out in its own moment of barbaric folly, the Gothic armies were, as usual, unrestrained, abandoned to passions, and generally given over to what Gibbon called "blind and irregular fury." Their "mischievous disposition" consumed with "improvident rage" the crops and the possessions of the local inhabitants. Eventually, an army of the Goths was surprised by the remaining Romans while "immersed in wine and sleep," and there followed in turn a "cruel slaughter of the astonished Goths." Thus, the anguish of the Barbaric Heart.

Is it too much to say that, a little more than a millennium and a half later, you could see the same surprise and anguish on the faces of the managers of international investment securities as the housing bubble burst and lenders, insurers, bond markets, and hedge funds all came close to evaporating as billions upon billions of dollars disappeared virtually overnight? All around them are the homeowners in foreclosure, just like the peasant villagers in 378 looking at the smoking ruins of their little homes.

The Barbaric Heart is a pure emptiness, an emptiness that doesn't know itself as empty. It is an emptiness that has turned upon itself. It is a mouth that chews. It is a permanent state of war against all others but also, most profoundly, against itself. One part violence, one part plunder, and eventual anguish and regret.

The Barbaric Heart cannot be punished for its excesses. It cannot be "shown the light of day." The proposals of the environmental community for better systems of transportation, cleaner smokestacks, purer foods, and jail time for corporate polluters—none of that changes the Barbaric Heart. If it is frustrated by the activities of others (those troublesome tree-huggers), it simply concludes that it will be more cunning and violent next time. As Nicholson Baker reports in his controversial book *Human Smoke,* in May of 1941 Lord Boom Trenchard considered the ineffectiveness of a year of daily bombing of the cities of Germany. What next? "Trenchard's answer was: *more.* More bombing. Relentless nightly bombing—heavier bombers, more bombers."

If the Barbaric Heart cannot be shown the errors of its ways, or even simply learn from its own tragic mistakes, then it must be displaced. That is, we should not seek to alter what the Barbaric Heart desires, for what it desires is what we desire: to be secure from outside threat, to protect its people (whether a tribe or a ruling class of elites), to thrive, to take pleasure in its world, etc. What we can do is make it seek by a new route what it constantly, unalterably seeks. What displaces the Barbaric Heart in this way is what I will call, for lack of a better term, thoughtfulness. (This is an inexact term, I know, but it has always been to the idea of "thinking" that philosophy has turned to confront the self-interest and violence of the barbaric. Thoughtfulness offers the Barbaric a better way to think about what it means to thrive.) In our current circumstances, thoughtfulness's first task is the acknowledgment that we have been lying to ourselves. Just about every aspect of what we happily call American culture is a form of

lie that we retell ourselves every day. The great virtue of Allen
Ginsberg's poem *Howl*, for example, was its determination
not to believe the lies of violence and avarice any longer. Its
prophetic howl erupted from a culture of mere consent. The
poem introduced an internal realignment of American culture
accomplished through what we now refer to as the countercul-
ture of the 1960s. The Barbaric Heart for a time stood naked
and exposed in its deceitfulness and violence. It was a "bright
shining lie," in Neil Sheehan's phrase. For a moment, the
usual logical appeals of economists and politicians for the ne-
cessity of violence and the supremacy of efficiency and profit
were found to be not only insufficient but morally repugnant.

In the end, the one important task of thoughtfulness is to
invent a spiritual principle, a logos of its own, that can contest the energies (and tyrannies) of the Barbaric Heart. But
thoughtfulness's primary attribute is not its ability to provide
a superior Truth or an irrefutable logic. Thoughtfulness's
primary attribute is aesthetic. That is, what thoughtfulness
proposes as an alternative to the self-serving violence of the
Barbaric is beauty. "Don't think profit," it argues, "think beauty. The beauty of the *polis*, the beauty of culture, the beauty of
human beings freed from the slavery of regimented work, and
the beauty of an untrammeled natural world." Through the
aesthetic, thoughtfulness seeks *Homo humanus* as opposed
to *Homo barbarus*. It seeks a culture in which humans can
become what they really are. Not slaves, and not instruments
of violence, but beings intent upon the beautiful as a social
principle. That's the logos of our better selves. And yet we
seem reluctant to claim it.

The idea that we are trying to create a culture whose primary satisfaction is its beauty is not really such an extravagant
thought. When we say that we desire a world in which nature
is intact and animal life thrives; when we say that we desire

human communities in harmony with nature; and when we
say that within those communities human beings should be
able to live in dignity, so that they can be something more
than worker-consumers, we are arguing for a reality that is
first aesthetic. Environmentalists argue for such a reality all
the time. It is what they propose in the place of a barbaric
culture of profit and violence. Even so, we are often seduced
by the economic and scientific appeals to efficiency, sustainability, and prosperity, in spite of the fact that we suspect that
these appeals are actually part of the problem. But in our heart
of hearts we are not fooled. What we want is the beautiful.
We say it with a smile on our faces when we go for a hike, or
when we visit an "eco-friendly" town full of bike paths and
locally owned shops with a mountain vista in the background.
We do not say of such places, "I'm grooving on this system's
ecological balance." Or, "The Green Economy is working
well." We say, "It's beautiful here!" And yet when we set out to
make our most public arguments for nature, we seem almost
embarrassed to say that what convinces us is the argument of
the beautiful. The *thoughtfulness* of the beautiful. In fact, I'm
embarrassed right now!

What is it that makes such an argument so difficult to
make? If what we want is the beautiful, why do we feel that our
most persuasive arguments will be made by scientists, environmental engineers, regional planners, and sustainability economists? In part, it is the fact that we have been intimidated by
all those who would say that such thinking is "unrealistic," by
which they really mean "does not concede the brutal fact of the
enduring triumph of the Barbaric Heart." By this measure, to
be realistic is to say, "We plan to win by conceding the game to
our adversaries before the contest has even begun."

Second perhaps only to toxic landscapes, the most thor-
oughly degraded aspect of our culture is its art. This is so

obvious that it hardly needs comment. One has simply to say "television." Nevertheless, it is art, or the aesthetic, that prohibits the temptation to mourn the death of the world we were born into. Art is not a call to passive contemplation (a trip to the museum) but to the activity of human creation. It is this that should replace Adam Smith's famous "division of labor," the work that promises only tedium and despair and passivity in the face of destruction. Environmentalism should be about a return to the aesthetic, and I don't mean the beauties of a mountain vista. I mean a resistance to the Barbaric Heart through a daily insistence on the Beautiful within individual lives, within communities, and in our relation to the natural world.

In Virgil's *Aeneid*, when Aeneas and the faithful Trojan remnant sail from Troy for the shores of Italy, they, in a sense, never leave Troy. They are never not Trojans because they take with them their "household gods," those figures and myths that provide them with identity. And when they land in Latium and begin to set up a new home, they do not feel themselves on strange shores. They are always at home. They bring the fullness of the past to meet the fullness of the present in productive beauty. By contrast, we're not even at home at home. We're strangers on our own shores, thanks to the way in which corporations and their franchises have colonized our cities and towns, turning them into one big McSame.

Historians often wonder what it was like for the Romans to live under the rule of the Goths in the sixth century. Barbarians in the Senate, barbarians in the market, barbarians in the temple, barbarians in the countryside. The constant presence of the violently alien. Well, perhaps it was like living with Best Buy and Costco and Barnes and Noble, in our Big Box world. In both the ancient world and the present, it is like living, in Nietzsche's mordant phrase, "estranged from house and home in the service of malignant dwarfs." But somehow when we look on the ugliness that this reality brings, we see a "high standard of living." Those enchanted by the malignant dwarfs (CEOs? MBAs?) do not think to ask, "What makes life worth living?" The answer is obvious: "The high standards, of course!" A very strange conclusion for a people who are the living witnesses of so much permanent destruction.

All of this is a roundabout way of saying that there is no need for environmentalism. Environmentalism has no victories to win. The very notion of environmentalism is not much more than a way of isolating a problem from its true context. The crisis of a degraded natural world is a part of the larger problem of the crisis of thought, the crisis of faith, and the crisis of the relation of human beings to Being (or God, if you prefer). What is called for is the discovery or invention of our own "household gods" that might speak powerfully to us. "Gods" that will keep us in touch with a sense of the depth of our own past and call us creatively to what we might call our primordial aesthetic passion: our deep desire to be the creators of our own world.

We ought to discover that there is something superior to the Barbaric Heart, a Universal that is not only Nature but human capacity and creativity as well. We ought to discover that we are a part of this One, an animal among animals. Ours should be a Dionysian world that refuses the cold comfort of both the capitalist manager and the ecologist technician. The Dionysian does not so much refuse these worlds as laugh in dismissal. Its world is indulgent and ecstatic and curiously impersonal. It is not an animal lover; it is simply happy among animals. It is not a nature lover; it is nature. It doesn't pity the plight of the polar bear; it romps in the snow. It is a thoughtful and beautiful animal, but it is an animal.

The Dionysian fucks, eats, looks for the ecstasy of transcendence, and worships the same gods that the animals worship. Not the God that gives laws, but the gods that encourage living things to thrive.

We are that strange and wonderful animal that has the metaphysical comfort of *knowing* that she is part of the tragic chorus of natural beings. We are members of that faith that knows that life is indestructibly powerful and pleasurable. And the mark that we will leave upon the world will not be the mark of brute force clothed in the false virtues of the barbarian but the mark of the ultimate realist, he who makes his own world, demanding the impossible and calling it Beautiful.

(2009)

BILL McKIBBEN

PIE IN THE SKY

Solutions to problems you never knew you had

QUESTION: should anyone who requires a "revolutionary new laser technology system" in order to figure out if they're parking in the right spot inside their own garage really be allowed behind the wheel in the first place? Compared with the other tasks of a driver—making right-hand turns, making left-hand turns, deciphering the red-amber-green vernacular of a stoplight—safely positioning your auto within the confines of your own garage seems like a fairly straightforward task, the kind of thing that might not require a laser. But you'd be surprised how useful lasers can be. The Hairmax Laser Comb, for instance, used only fifteen minutes a day, three times a week, results in noticeably thicker locks and tresses. And not just lasers. Ions are also surprisingly useful—confusingly, negative ions. A lamp made of salt crystal mined from the Himalayas emits them, aiding you in the fight against "dust mites" and also "depression."

If there's any piece of writing that defines our culture, I submit it's the SkyMall catalogue, available in the seatback pocket of every airplane in North America. To browse its pages is to understand the essential secret of American consumer life: we've officially run out not only of things that we need, but even of things that we might plausibly desire. But we in the airline traveling class still have a few problems to solve in our lives. Judging from the joys on offer, our particular worries at the moment might be categorized as follows:

I'm overworked and overtired. In which case, I need a $4,000 massaging recliner with voice control, synthetic leather ("softer, more plush than leather"), and thirty-three airbags—a machine that "pampers your body and soothes your soul." And if perchance I drift off to sleep, "the peaceful progression wake-up clock" will rouse me with infinite care. "Thirty minutes before wake-up time, the light glows softly, brightening over the next half hour, while faint aromatherapy scents release into the air. Fifteen minutes before wake up, the clock generates one of six soft nature sounds." In case that isn't quite enough, I might want to back it up with the "sensory assault alarm clock," whose large, wired vibrating pad placed under the mattress shakes you awake in time to turn off the clock before it emits a ninety-five-decibel alarm and starts flashing a strobe light.

I have an immense supply of trousers, and hence require the closet organizer trouser rack to keep twenty pairs of slacks neatly hung and readily accessible. The five-eighths-inch-diameter birch dowels "reduce creasing of even fine fabrics," and "nylon washers between the dowels ensure smooth swing motion."

I distrust my neighbors and my government, and so would benefit from a giant-capacity mailbox that holds up to two weeks of mail (catalogues, presumably). "Don't bother a neighbor to get your mail, and don't tell the post office you'll be away."

I am extremely, extremely clean. I'm therefore thankful that my toothbrush has been ultravioletly cleansed overnight to remove the "millions of germs" that would otherwise accumulate, and my room is protected against "airborne bacteria, viruses, and germs" by a Germ Guardian machine, "proven by a Harvard researcher," which "takes ultraviolet C energy and multiplies its germ-killing power in our exclusive Intensifier Chamber." Also, I have another very similar-looking machine "now with exclusive Ozoneguard" in case any ozone is nearby. And a soap dispenser with infrared sensor technology for my shower, a "no-touch approach that dramatically reduces the chance of spreading germs."

I have way too many watches, and therefore might benefit from a $300 case that will shake them all with "intermittent timers and directional controls" to mimic the action of a human wrist and hence keep them fully wound at all times.

I have plugged in so many things that the planet has warmed considerably, reducing the chances that my children will experience a natural winter. So I have purchased a "weatherproof light projection box that rests on your front lawn and transforms the entire facade of your house into an illuminated snowscape. The box creates the illusion of gently falling snow flurries by directing a bright white beam onto a rotating mirrorball." Flake size and fall rate are, pleasingly, adjustable. I have opted also to purchase an "exclusive heavy duty vinyl snow castle" that will "set up almost anywhere in just minutes with the included electric pump." A real snow castle would, SkyMall notes, "take hours to build and require lots of snow," but this version "encourages children to use their imaginations while having fun."

I have an enormous number of remote controls, and hence need caddies to store them, small "buddy lights" to illuminate them, and locator devices to find them when I have mislaid them.

I may be devolving. Though for eons my ancestors have

grilled meat over flames, I am no longer very clear on the concept and so would like a digital barbecue fork that I can stick into my burger or steak and receive a readout indicating whether it is currently rare, medium, or well done. Also, it would help a lot to have all the lights already strung on my artificial Christmas tree, and the difficult task of marinating would be much easier if I had a $199.95 marinating machine. Frankly, I've lately found grilled cheese sandwiches more trouble than I want, but with my dishwasher-safe Toastabag I can simply place a slice of cheese between two slices of bread and pop it in my toaster. (Depressing the toaster lever still requires my thoughtful attention, as does chewing the resulting treat.)

There are a few problems SkyMall can't solve (the lack of community that comes when you live in a giant stuff-filled house marooned on its half-acre lot, the lack of security that comes when your country is spending its money on remote-control golf balls instead of, say, healthcare and retirement savings). And there's always the vexing question of what the people who are making these items think about the people who will buy them. (I was in a shower curtain factory in rural China last year where the very nice people sewing the curtains told another visitor that they'd never actually encountered a shower curtain outside the factory. If that's true for a shower curtain, one wonders what their fellow workers make of the traveling wine trolley, the pop-up hot dog cooker, the hand-held paper shredder with wood-grain plastic handle.)

But this kind of talk sounds tired, clichéd, left over from the '60s. Everyone knows that the most important thing we can do is grow the economy. When you buy the Designated Driver, a faux golf club that you store in your bag to dispense forty-eight ounces of cold beverages, then you grow the economy. No doubt about it. Also, the Vintage Express Aging Accelerator that ages your bottle of wine ten years in ten seconds by surrounding it with "extremely powerful Neodymium magnets to replicate the Earth's magnetic field." Only a real jerk or a Christian or something would point out that there might possibly be items in this world that it would make more sense to spend our money on. (Insecticide-impregnated bednets to stop the spread of malaria run about five dollars. If only they came in self-erecting pastel versions that would also rouse you out of bed with gentle nature sounds.)

(2006)

WINONA LADUKE

RICEKEEPERS

A struggle to protect biodiversity and a Native American way of life

AS FALL TEMPERATURES CHANGE on the White Earth Reservation and the mist lifts off the lakes, the Ojibwe take to the waters. Two people to a canoe, one poles through the thick rice beds, pushing the canoe forward, while the other, sitting toward the front of the boat, uses two long sticks to gently bend the rice and knock the seeds into the canoe. The sounds of *manoominike*, the wild rice harvest, are the gliding of the boat through the water and across shafts of rice, the soft *swish* of the rice bending, the raining of the rice into the canoe. They are soothing sounds, reminding my people of the continuity between the generations. We have been harvesting rice here for centuries.

Each year, my family and I join hundreds of other harvesters who return daily with hundreds of pounds of rice from the region's lakes and rivers. We call it the Wild Rice Moon, Manoominike Giizis. On White Earth, Leech Lake, Nett Lake, and other Ojibwe reservations in the Great Lakes region, it is a time when people harvest a food to feed their bellies and to sell for *zhooniyaash*, or cash, to meet basic expenses. But it is also a time to feed the soul.

Fifteen hundred miles away, in Woodland, California, a company called Nor-Cal has received a patent on wild rice. Conceptually, it seems almost impossible—patenting something called *wild* rice. The Ojibwe now find themselves at the center of an international battle over who owns lifeforms, foods, and medicines that have throughout history been the collective property of indigenous peoples.

An estimated 90 percent of the world's biodiversity lies within the territories of indigenous peoples, whether the Amazon, the Indian subcontinent, or the North Woods. A new form of colonialism, known as biocolonialism, is reaching deep into the heart of these communities. As Stephanie Howard wrote for the Indigenous People's Council on Biocolonialism, "The flow of genes is primarily from indigenous communities and rural communities in 'developing countries' to the Northern-based genetics industry. Ninety-seven percent of all patents are held by industrialized countries."

In 1994, for example, two researchers at the University of Colorado were able to secure a patent on quinoa, much to the surprise of native farmers in the Andean region of Bolivia and Ecuador who had been cultivating and stewarding the grain for thousands of years. The patent gave the university exclusive control over a traditional Bolivian sterile male variety called Apelawa, and also extended to hybrids developed from the breeding of forty-three additional traditional varieties. In 1998, the Bolivian National Quinoa Producers Association, with support from other groups internationally, was able to convince the researchers to drop the patent. But similar patents were issued on the neem tree, ayahuasca (a medicinal plant of the Amazon), and many other medicinal plants. Some of these were also eventually revoked. In September 1997, RiceTec, a Texas-based company, even won a controversial patent on the famed basmati rice. When the Indian government filed a complaint with the U.S. Patent and Trademark Office, RiceTec was forced to give up fifteen of twenty patent claims.

It was within this climate that University of Minnesota plant geneticist Ron Phillips, along with a few colleagues, mapped the wild rice genome in 2000. According to Phillips, this work is considered "important as a foundation for genetic and crop improvement studies." The Ojibwe believe that these studies, bearing names such as "Molecular Cytogenetics in Plant Improvement," could have far-reaching implications. The wild rice gene map is now filed with GenBank, a database operated by the National Institutes of Health, and its availability essentially sets the stage for genetic modification.

Traditional breeding techniques attempt to enhance certain traits of the wild rice and to repress others, but with genetic engineering, it becomes possible to insert DNA from other plants into the wild rice. The Ojibwe are alarmed by this possibility, viewing it as an attack on the essential nature of the rice itself.

Thousands of years ago, according to our oral histories, the Anishinaabeg—called the Ojibwe or Chippewa by the federal government—followed a shell in the sky from the great waters of the East to the place where the food grows on the water. That food was wild rice, the only grain indigenous to North America, and it has been a central food in ceremony and sustenance for our people ever since. "The[y] gain their livelihood by fishing, hunting, gathering berries and wild rice and making maple sugar, which constitutes their chief means of support," Indian agents would write, noting that the Ojibwe also relied on wild rice as a source of trade with the white settlers, and later as a source of credit and cash.

The rice was so significant to the Ojibwe that the lands with the best wild rice stands—including Big Rice Lake, Rice Lake Refuge, Lake Winnibigoshish, Nett Lake, and other mother lodes of the great grain—were reserved. Beyond the reservation borders, land was transferred to the U.S. government, but the rice was not. In an 1837 treaty, the Ojibwe ceded nearly 14 million acres of Wisconsin and Minnesota but retained "the privilege of hunting, fishing, and gathering the wild rice upon the lands, the rivers and the lakes included in the territory ceded." Federal and Supreme Court cases, including the 1999 Mille Lacs Supreme Court case, have upheld the rights of the Ojibwe to traditional land-use outside the reservations.

It was this close bond between a people and a food that University of Minnesota professor Albert Jenks encountered when he came to White Earth and other reservations to study wild rice in the late 1800s. He noted with disdain the Ojibwe harvesting practices. "Wild rice, which had led to their advance thus far, held them back from further progress," he determined. His perception of the Ojibwe wild rice harvest as a bastion of primitiveness would become the prevailing opinion at the University of Minnesota throughout the twentieth century—indeed, a sort of battle cry for industrializing agriculture.

In the 1950s, University of Minnesota researchers decided it was time to liberate the rice from the indigenous people. So they set out to domesticate wild rice. A university scientist named Ervin Oelke began the process, using germ plasm collected from twenty-four natural stands within the 1837 treaty area. Over the years, the Minnesota Agricultural Extension office was able to "create" several strains of "wild" rice: Johnson in 1968, M1 in 1970, M2 in 1972, M3 in 1974, Netum in 1978,

Voyager in 1983, Meter in 1985, Franklin in 1992, and Purple Petrowski in 2000.

In effect, what the Creator gave to the Anishinaabeg has become a profit-making enterprise for others. These domesticated varieties are engineered to ripen at the same time and, with a harder hull, can be harvested mechanically. They are cultivated in paddies, flooded fields that are drained to allow access with a combine. By 1968, Minnesota's paddy wild rice production already represented some 20 percent of the state's yield. This increase in production, along with growing national demand for wild rice and subsequent interest from corporations such as Uncle Ben's, Green Giant, and General Foods, permanently altered the market for traditionally harvested wild rice. Lake rice could no longer compete with the mass-manufactured paddy crop. The wholesale wild rice price dropped from $4.44 per pound in 1967 to $2.68 a pound in 1976, destabilizing the wild rice economy of the Ojibwe.

Then, in 1977, the Minnesota state legislature designated wild rice the official state grain—a tragic turn of events for the lake harvest. With an outpouring from the state coffers, the University of Minnesota began to aggressively market a domesticated version of wild rice. By the early 1980s paddy-grown wild rice had outstripped the indigenous varieties in production.

Ironically, greed knows no state boundaries. Minnesota lost control over production of its official state grain to California, which by 1983 produced over 8.3 million pounds, compared to Minnesota's 5 million pounds. By 1986, more than 95 percent of the wild rice harvested was paddy grown, the vast majority produced in California. As this glut of wild rice hit the market, prices plummeted. Many Ojibwe lost their source of livelihood. But to add insult to injury, many of the paddy rice companies were selling their product as if it were *wild* wild rice, in some cases even using Ojibwe images in their advertising.

The Ojibwe fought back. In 1988, *Wabizii v. Busch Agricultural Resources*, a lawsuit on the issue of false and misleading advertising, was filed. Busch Agricultural Resources (a division of the beer conglomerate) was marketing a product called Onamia Wild Rice, which plaintiffs Mike Swan and Frank Bibeau charged was in fact a California-grown paddy product disguised as Minnesota lake rice. "They had two Indians on a canoe who appeared to be picking wild rice. They were taking a California-grown product, trucking it to Minnesota, where it was packaged and designated as a Minnesota product," Bibeau, a White Earth tribal member, recalls. The case was settled out of court, and eventually the state passed a law forcing paddy wild-rice producers to label their product as such, with the words "paddy rice" no less than half the size of the words "wild rice." Still, the Minnesota labeling law does not apply to California-grown wild rice, so three-quarters of the nation's domesticated crop can be described as "wild" without qualification.

Wild rice, or *Zizania palustris*, is actually a grass, sharing only some genetic traits with other rice crops internationally. The differences in wild rice beds are well known to local harvesters. Some plants grow tall and live in deep water; others have adapted to shallow water. Some strains have fat grains; others have long grains. They range in color from purple to light brown to greenish. That biodiversity is the staff of life, and it is essential to the security of the rice. That same biodiversity served as the genetic basis for the domesticated varieties, an agricultural monocrop.

The Anishinaabeg believe there is a real possibility that wild rice stands could be contaminated by the domesticated varieties. There are around six thousand bodies of water with significant wild rice beds in Minnesota, containing around sixty thousand acres of rice. And there are around twenty thousand acres of cultivated wild rice paddies in close proximity to most of those native beds. Ron Phillips claims there is little chance of cross-pollination as long as approximately 660 feet separate the two kinds of wild rice. However, in the summer of 2002, university researchers noted the possibility of between 1 and 5 percent of the pollen from test plots drifting up to two miles.

Then there is, in Donald Rumsfeld's vernacular, the unknown unknown of the *zhiishiibig*, the ducks. Ducks and other waterfowl do not differentiate between paddy rice plots and natural stands of wild rice; they move freely between them, carrying rice from one to the other. Phillips himself acknowledges a problem: "It depends on what you are willing to accept as a threshold of risk. You can't guarantee . . . that a bird won't pick up a weed and take it twenty miles away," he said.

As for Nor-Cal Wild Rice, U.S. patent number 5955648 secures its rights to a traditional breeding process which uses something known as "cytoplasmic genetic male sterility" to produce hybrid varieties. John Pershell of the Water Quality Research Department of the Minnesota Chippewa Tribe read all thirty pages of the patent. "Nowhere did it mention anything about the wild rice being wild or coming from somewhere," he said. The rice has basically been co-opted. But what's worse, those confusing words, "cytoplasmic genetic male sterility," are essentially a fancy way of saying that these varieties cannot reproduce. They are sterile. The Ojibwe are concerned that, like the notorious "terminator" seeds, Nor-Cal's strain of wild rice could negatively affect the vitality of wild lake rice.

These fears were validated by two major contamination incidents in August 2006. In the first, genetically engineered bentgrass escaped its testing ground in Oregon. Three years earlier, farmers had joined with environmentalists and the Center for Food Safety in pursuing a lawsuit against the USDA, which had, in their assessment, failed to properly regulate varieties of creeping bentgrass and Kentucky blue-grass that had been genetically engineered to resist the weed-killer Roundup. In February 2007, U.S. District Judge Henry H. Kennedy Jr. ruled in favor of the plaintiffs, citing evidence that field tests had the potential to be harmful to other crops, and instructing the USDA to cease approval for field tests of genetically engineered crops until it can give more scrutiny to applications.

Last August as well, news was released that a German company was responsible for the contamination of a vast portion of the U.S. long-grain white rice crop by a genetically engineered variety never intended for human consumption. When the news spread, European and Asian markets began strictly limiting their importation of all U.S. long-grain white rice. Japan banned the white rice crop outright. The European Union demanded that expensive genetic tests be conducted to guarantee no presence of genetically engineered organisms. Rice futures prices tumbled $150 million in a single day and rice exports are estimated to decline by as much as 16 percent in 2007. Following this fiasco, farmers from Arkansas, Missouri, Mississippi, Louisiana, Texas, and California filed a lawsuit against Bayer CropScience, charging the corporation with tainting the domestic crop and damaging the U.S. export market. Industry responded by filing a petition to deregulate its untested, genetically engineered product. Meanwhile, scientists are still trying to figure out how an experimental crop that was discontinued years ago, and was apparently grown at distances beyond what the USDA considered adequate to prevent contamination, managed to become commingled with long-grain white rice harvested from many different locations.

Though no one has yet attempted to grow genetically engineered wild rice in the out-of-doors, a similar contamination scenario would be devastating. Tainted lake rice would be virtually unable to compete in international markets, and over half of all wild rice is sold internationally.

For the past nine years, the Anishinaabeg community has repeatedly requested that the University of Minnesota stop its genetic work on wild rice. "We object to the exploitation of our wild rice for pecuniary gain," wrote Minnesota Chippewa Tribal President Norman Deschampe in a 1998 letter to the University of Minnesota. He continued: "We are of the opinion that the wild rice rights assured by treaty accrue not only to individual grains of rice, but to the very essence of the resource. We were not promised just any wild rice; that promise could be kept by delivering sacks of grain to our members each year. We were promised the rice that grew in the waters of our people, and all the value that rice holds."

In September 2003, a coalition of Ojibwe tribal governments and members demanded the following concessions from the university: a moratorium on genomic research and genetic research on wild rice at the university, to be effective December 31, 2004; protection of Anishinaabeg intellectual property rights to wild rice, including a ban on selling these rights; a cultural consultation program to be set in place by the university to examine the ethics of research on cross-cultural issues; and mutually agreed upon beneficial research to be done on behalf of Anishinaabeg people, equal to that done on behalf of the cultivated wild-rice industry. A satisfactory response is still pending. More recently, the White Earth and Fond du Lac bands of Ojibwe have adopted ordinances banning the genetic modification of wild rice, following the lead of several California counties and a host of international ordinances on GMOs.

In the spring of 2006, a letter signed by over seventy Minnesota state legislators promoting the protection of wild rice was secured by state representative Frank Moe, whose constituents include two Ojibwe bands, but only after a pitched battle with the biotech industry and the University of Minnesota. At the legislative hearings, representatives for both the industry and the university testified against protecting wild rice from genetic engineering, pushing instead for an open-door policy for the future. Biotech giant Monsanto, unsurprisingly, argued that such protection would send a "chilling message" to the biotech industry, and perhaps diminish its investment in the state.

Despite this opposition, a protection bill for wild rice was signed into law in early May 2007. The legislation requires that any entity wanting to grow genetically engineered wild rice in Minnesota must file an environmental impact statement with the state. It also requires that state entities notify the tribes of any permits granted to grow genetically engineered wild rice in other states, and that they engage in studies to better understand the threat that genetic engineering poses to wild rice.

The controversy over wild rice is similar to a recent dispute over taro, a sacred food of Native Hawaiians. Since January 2006, Hawaiians had been pressuring the University of Hawai'i to give up patents it held on three varieties of taro, arguing that taro, the "elder brother" of Native Hawaiians, should not be subject to transgenic experimentation. Gary Ostrander, vice-chancellor for research and graduate education at the University of Hawai'i at Manoa, describes how the three disease-resistant taro strains were created after a leaf blight wiped out 90 percent of Samoan taro in the 1990s. University scientists had used traditional breeding techniques to cross Palauan and Hawaiian taro, and the university had obtained plant patents on the resulting strains in 2002. However, after negotiations with Native Hawaiian taro farmers and legal counsel, the university fled "terminal disclaimers" with the U.S. Patent Office, dissolving its proprietary interests. And in June 2006, the university literally tore up its patents. "It is as if the patents were never filed," said Ostrander in an article in the *Honolulu Star-Bulletin*, adding that he had come to appreciate the Native Hawaiians' point of view on the issue.

Earlier that spring, the pueblos of New Mexico had joined with Hispanic communities in a historic declaration of seed sovereignty, reaffirming seed-saving traditions and rejecting patents and genetically engineered seed. The declaration states that the traditional farmers of Indo-Hispano and Native-American ancestry in northern New Mexico "consider genetic modification and the potential contamination of our landraces by GE technology a continuation of genocide upon indigenous people and as malicious and sacrilegious acts toward our ancestry, culture, and future generations." In October 2006, the declaration was passed by the National Congress of American Indians, an organization comprised of the elected tribal leadership of federally recognized tribes. And in early 2007, the New Mexico state legislature passed a memorial "recognizing the significance of indigenous agricultural practices and native seeds to New Mexico's cultural heritage and food security." Even though several clauses concerning the threat of genetic engineering were deleted due to pressure from Monsanto and the State Department of Agriculture, the final version resolved that the House of Representatives "supports efforts to prevent genetic contamination of native seeds."

Rowen White, a Mohawk seed saver and farmer, explains

what's at stake: "A cultural community that persists in its farming tradition does not simply conserve indigenous seed stock because of economic justifications. The seeds themselves become symbols, reflections of the peoples' own spiritual and aesthetic identity, and of the land that shaped them."

"We stand to lose everything," says White Earth tribal member Joe LaGarde, who has harvested wild rice since he was a small child. "If we lose our rice, we won't exist as a people for long." This is why tribal entities in the North Country are determined to differentiate the wild rice that is harvested from lakes and rivers from the corporatized version, and are seeking national and international markets for their rarefied product. Through work that is somewhat like the fair-trade struggle of coffee farmers, the Ojibwe are beginning to regain an economic foothold with the wild rice economy. The key is to keep the rice and protect it; to remain connected to a traditional way of life and the land.

It was in that spirit that I took my fifteen-year-old son out ricing on the Ottertail River last year, far from the din of television, Game Boys, NASCAR, and big cities. I let him pole for the first time. He's quite a bit larger than I, and in the past I would do the poling out of fear that he would dump the boat—and his mother—into the lake. But over time he's become more steady, and I've become more docile. We watched the *wabiziwag*, the trumpeter swans, lift off the river and listened to the sound of rice falling in the canoe.

There is something irreplaceable about following the canoe path of your ancestors through the rice beds. It's sort of a miracle in this millennium that this age-old tradition continues. But it does. And it will.

Apane. Always.

(2007)

SANDRA STEINGRABER

3 BETS

On ecology, economy, and human health

THIRTY YEARS AGO, in between my sophomore and junior
years of college, I was diagnosed with bladder cancer. Those
are amazing words to write: *Thirty years ago I had cancer.* I
had just turned twenty. I was hoping that I would live long
enough to have sex with someone; I hadn't done that yet.
I could not have imagined, while lying in my hospital bed,
exhaling anesthesia, that someday I could write, *Thirty years
ago I had cancer.*

Last fall, on a sunny afternoon, the phone rang while I
was trying to meet a writing deadline. It was the nurse in my
urologist's office. She was calling to say that the pathologist
had found, in the urine collected from my last cystoscopic
checkup, abnormal cell clusters. And also blood.

After I hung up, I looked out the window of my small
house where the sun still shone on the last of the marigolds
and tomato vines. I looked down at my computer screen
where the cursor still blinked on the same paragraph. I could
hear in the kitchen the tomatoes still bobbing around in the
stockpot that was steaming away on the stove. The world was
still the same, but it felt to me a suddenly altered place.

I provided a second urine sample for further testing, and based on the results of that, a third sample that was sent out for genetic analysis. Ten days later, I got a call from the urology nurse. The results were normal.

So what am I trying to say here? Am I fine or not fine? Well, I don't know. I'm living within that period of time known as watchful waiting. Much of my adult life has been one of watchful waiting. *Watchful* means vigilance, screening tests, imaging, blood work, self-advocacy, second opinions, and hours logged in hospital parking garages. *Waiting* means you go back to your half-finished essay, to the tomatoes on the stove. You lay plans and carry on within the confines of ambiguity. You meet deadlines and make grocery lists. And sometimes you jump when the phone rings on a sunny afternoon.

Thirty years ago I had cancer.

After I left the hospital, I went back to the university, resumed my life as a biology major, and began mucking around in the medical literature. It didn't take me too long to learn that bladder cancer is considered a quintessential environmental cancer, meaning that we have more evidence for a link between toxic chemical exposures and bladder cancer risk than for almost any other kind of cancer, with data going back a hundred years. I also discovered that the identification of bladder carcinogens does not preclude their ongoing use in commerce. Just because, through careful scientific study, we learn that a chemical causes cancer doesn't mean that we ban it from the marketplace.

I also learned that, in spite of all this evidence, the words *carcinogen* and *environment* rarely appeared in the pamphlets on cancer in my doctors' offices and waiting rooms. Nor were these words used much in conversations I had with my various health-care providers, who were interested instead in my family medical history. I was happy enough to provide it. There is a lot of cancer in my family. My mother was diagnosed with breast cancer at age forty-four. I have uncles with colon cancer, prostate cancer, stromal cancer. My aunt died of the same kind of bladder cancer—transitional cell carcinoma—that I had.

But here's the punch line to my family story: I am adopted. I'm not related to my family by chromosomes. So I began to ask hard questions about the presumption that what runs in families must necessarily run in genes. I began to ask, what else do families have in common? Such as, say, drinking water wells. And when I looked at the literature on cancer among adult adoptees, I learned that, in fact, the chance of an adopted person dying of cancer is closely related to whether or not her adoptive parents had died of cancer and far less related to whether or not her biological parents had met such a fate. But you would never know that based on the questions asked on medical intake forms.

So thirty years ago, as a college undergraduate, I made a bet. I bet that my cancer diagnosis had something to do with the environment in which I lived as a child. And I think I was right about this.

As I learned years later, while researching my book *Living Downstream*, the county where I grew up, along the east bluff of the Illinois River, has statistically elevated cancer rates. Three dozen different industries line the river valley there, and farmers practice chemically intensive agriculture along its floodplains. Hazardous waste is imported from as far away as New Jersey, and the drinking water wells contain traces of both farm chemicals and industrial chemicals, including those with demonstrable links to . . . bladder cancer.

Twenty years ago, in the fall of 1988, when I was a graduate student in biology at the University of Michigan, I made another bet. I was working as an opinion writer at the *Michigan*

Daily, the student newspaper there. My editor and I laid bets as to which system would collapse first—economy or ecology. I said ecology. I think I was wrong.

I think we were both wrong. They seem to be crumbling simultaneously.

Let's compare our twin "eco" systems. Our economy and our ecology have in common, it seems to me, a number of shared attributes. Both are complex, globalized systems whose interconnections are little understood until something goes wrong. Who knew that mortgages in California could lead to bankruptcy in Iceland? But there it is. Who knew that the miracle of pollination depends on the synchronicity of time and temperature? But the ongoing decoupling of day length—which awakens the flowers—from ambient temperature—which awakens the bees—reveals that it is so dependent.

In both systems, eroding diversity creates fragility, as when financial systems merge and collapse, as when farming systems become monocultures and thereby vulnerable to catastrophic pest outbreaks. Damage to both systems is made worse by positive feedback loops. In the economic world, panic and fear drive investment decisions that lead to more panic and fear. In the ecological world, greenhouse gases raise temperatures that melt permafrost. Melted permafrost rots and releases more greenhouse gases.

Here's a key difference, though. For one of our failing eco-systems, we became immediately engaged in drastic and unprecedented measures to rescue it—even though no one seemed to understand it very well. And for our other eco-system . . . well, it's still widely considered too depressing and overwhelming to talk about in much detail.

As part of my work, I visit a lot of college campuses. Lately, I've been asking students to engage in a thought exercise: Imagine that ecological metrics were as familiar to us as economic ones. Imagine ecological equivalents to the Dow, NASDAQ, and S&P that reported to us every day—in newspapers, on radio, on websites, on the crawl at the bottom of TV screens, on oversized tickers in Times Square—data about the various sectors of our ecological system and how they are faring. What are the atmospheric parts per million of carbon dioxide today? Has the extinction rate become inflationary? What is the exchange rate between sea ice and fresh water? What is the national deficit of topsoil?

Now imagine that the mainstream media were as interested in the thoughts of the president's ecological team—most notably marine biologist Jane Lubchenco, who now leads the National Oceanic and Atmospheric Administration, and climate expert John Holdren, the president's new science advisor—as they are in the opinions of his economic team. Imagine if, in primetime interview after interview, these public servants provided us regular environmental analysis. On an almost daily basis, the American citizenry would be reminded that one in every four mammals now appears to be heading toward extinction. The Gulf Stream, which drives nutrient cycling in our oceans, is starting to get wobbly, while dead zones in the oceans are growing. The oceans, we would be informed, provide half of our planetary oxygen. Shoveling coal into ovens to generate electricity is loading the atmosphere with mercury, which rains down and is transformed by ancient bacteria into the powerful brain poison methylmercury. Methylmercury is siphoned up the food chain, concentrating as it goes, so that nearly all freshwater lakes and streams east of the Mississippi are now unfishable, and we must advise women and children against eating tuna salad sandwiches.

Imagine that all Americans find out, whether they want to or not, that atmospheric loading of carbon dioxide is acidifying the ocean in ways that, if unchecked, will drop pH to the point where calcium carbonate goes into solution, and that will spell the end of anything with a shell—from clams and oysters to coral reefs.

Suppose that ecological pundits discussed every night on cable TV the ongoing disappearance of bees, bats, and other pollinators and the possibly dire consequences for our food supply. Suppose we received daily reports on the status of our aquifers. Suppose legislators and citizens both agreed that if we don't take immediate action to bail out our ecological system, something truly terrible will happen. Our ecology will tank.

The fact that nothing close to this is happening is the difference between economy and ecology, both of which share an etymology: *eco*, from the Greek *oikos*, meaning "household."

Ten years ago, I gave birth to a child. After twenty years as a solitary adult ecologist, I became a habitat, an inland ocean with a marine mammal swimming around inside of me. I became a water cycle. A food chain. A jet stream. My daughter's name is Faith. I'll leave it to you to imagine why an adopted cancer survivor might name a daughter Faith. My daughter is planning a career as a marine biologist. She wants to write her first book on the octopus. My son Elijah is seven. He is named for the abolitionist Elijah Lovejoy, who hails from my home state of Illinois. Elijah wishes to be the president, a farmer, or a member of the Beatles. He figures there are two job openings there already.

Since becoming a mother, I've made another bet. I am betting that, in between my own adult life and my children's, an environmental human rights movement will arise. It's one whose seeds have already been sown, and it's one with a dual focus. First, the environmental human rights movement will take up with urgency the task of rescuing and repairing our ecological system upon which all human life depends. It is a movement that will recognize the truth of the following statement: "Nothing is more important to human beings than an ecologically functioning, life sustaining biosphere on the Earth. . . . We cannot live long or well without a functioning biosphere, and so it is worth everything we have." Those are the opening sentences of a powerful new manifesto, "Law for the Ecological Age," authored by attorney and biochemist Joseph Guth and published in the *Vermont Journal of Environmental Law.*

At the same time, this environmental human rights movement will take up with equal fervor the task of divorcing our economy from its current dependencies on chemical toxicants that are known to trespass inside our bodies, without our consent, thus violating, as some have argued, our security of person. Our current environmental regulatory apparatus does not require rigorous toxicological testing of chemicals as a precondition for marketing them, as we do, for example, for pharmaceuticals. It also makes it very difficult to ban chemicals once they are in commerce. Of the eighty thousand synthetic chemicals allowed into the market, exactly five have been outlawed under the Toxics Substances Control Act since 1976. Our current environmental regulatory apparatus allows economic benefits to be balanced against human health risks. It fails to take into account the fact that we are all exposed, to use Rachel Carson's words, to a changing kaleidoscope of chemicals over our lifetimes and not just one chemical at a time.

In umbilical cord blood alone, 287 different chemicals have been identified, including pesticides, stain removers, wood preservatives, mercury, and flame retardants. Our current environmental regulatory apparatus does not take into account the timing of exposure. And yet the science clearly shows that toxic exposures during key moments of infant and child development—especially during the opera of embryonic development—raise risks for harm in ways that are not predictable by dose. Benzo[a]pyrene, an ingredient in tobacco smoke, diesel exhaust, and soot, can damage eggs in the ovaries. Exposure to pesticides in men can reduce sperm count. Thus, our environmental policies may be eroding our fertility. And if a pregnancy is achieved, exposure to certain chemicals raises the risk that it will be lost through miscarriage, or what we in the scientific community call spontaneous abortion. Evidence suggests that the pesticide methoxchlor has this power, as do certain chemical solvents.

And here is where I am interested in engaging the pro-life community in dialogue, because whether you see this problem, as I do, as a violation of women's reproductive rights, or whether you see this problem, as many members of my own family do, as a violation of fetal sanctity, maybe we can all agree, pro-life and pro-choice, that any chemical with the power to extinguish human pregnancy has no rightful place in our economy.

When toxic chemicals enter the story of human development during the fifth and sixth months of pregnancy, when the brain is just getting itself knitted together, the risk may be a learning or developmental disability. Of the 3,000 chemicals produced in high volume in the United States, 200 are neurotoxicants and another 1,000 are suspected of affecting the nervous system.

Some chemicals, such as PCBs, have the power to shorten human gestation and so raise the risk for premature birth, which is the leading cause of disability in this country. After birth, some chemicals, such as certain air pollutants, can retard the development of the lungs in ways that impede later athletic performance. Some chemicals raise the risk for pediatric cancers, which are rising in incidence more rapidly than cancers among adults. Some chemicals can raise the risk for early puberty in girls, which in turn raises the risk for breast cancer in adulthood. In short, chemical toxicants can sabotage the story of child development and so make urgent the need for restructuring our chemicals policy along the principles of precaution and green design. But toxic chemicals do not only discriminate against children, they may also discriminate against our elders. New evidence links environmental exposures to neurotoxicants to increased risks of dementing disorders in old age.

So I am betting that chemical reform will be a cornerstone of this new environmental human rights movement that I see getting under way. I am betting that my children—and the generation of children they are a part of—will, by the time they are my age, consider it unthinkable to allow cancer-causing chemicals, reproductive toxicants, and brain-destroying poisons to freely circulate in our economy. They will find it unthinkable to assume an attitude of silence and willful ignorance about our ecology.

In the same way, I look back on the life of Rachel Carson—my mentor in all this, who died when I was five years old—and find it unthinkable that she could not speak about her own cancer diagnosis, even while dying, as I have written about my diagnosis here. Thirty years of feminism lies between my life as an adult scientist and Rachel Carson's. That human rights movement has ended the silence around the personal experience of cancer so that I have never had to fear, as did Carson, that my status as a cancer survivor will be used to impeach my science.

And in the same way, I look back on the life of Abraham Lincoln, whose portrait hangs in every schoolroom in Illinois, and marvel that our economy was once dependent on slave labor. Unthinkable. I believe our grandchildren will look back on us and marvel that our economy was once dependent on chemicals that were killing the planet and killing ourselves.

Now I am willing to concede the point that this environmental human rights movement that I am betting on is less an evidence-based prediction than a mother's fervent hope that my children will never have to fear that the phone ringing on a sunny afternoon will bring bad news from the pathology lab. I'm willing to admit that this bet is a wish that my children will grow up in a world with a functioning Gulf Stream, and some ice caps, and a few coral reefs. And some octopi for my daughter to write her first book about. And some honeybees to help my son the farmer grow apples. It's a wish that his polar bear Halloween costume not outlast the species.

Wishful or not, I am determined to win this bet because my children's lives are inextricably bound to the abiding ecology of this planet, which is worth everything I could possibly wager. An environmental human rights movement is the vision under which I labor, from which I am not free to desist, and which may, if we all work together, become a self-fulfilling prophecy.

May it be so.

(2009)

CONTRIBUTORS

Jeff Goodell is the author of, most recently, *How to Cool the Planet: Geoengineering and the Audacious Quest to Fix Earth's Climate,* which won the 2011 Grantham Prize Award of Special Merit. As a commentator on energy and environmental issues, he has appeared on NPR, MSNBC, CNN, CNBC, ABC, NBC, PBS, *Fox News,* and *The Oprah Winfrey Show.*

James Gustave Speth, currently a professor at Vermont Law School, was formerly dean of the Yale School of Forestry & Environmental Studies. He cofounded the Natural Resources Defense Council, was founder and president of the World Resources Institute, and served as administrator of the United Nations Development Programme. He is the author of six books, including the award-winning *Bridge at the Edge of the World: Capitalism, the Environment, and Crossing from Crisis to Sustainability.*

Derrick Jensen is the author of numerous books, including *Endgame, The Culture of Make Believe,* and *A Language Older than Words.* He was named one of *Utne Reader*'s "50 Visionaries Who Are Changing Your World" and won the Eric Hoffer Award in 2008. He writes for *Audubon, The Sun,* and many other publications.

Jeffrey Kaplan has long been an activist in the Bay Area. His articles have appeared in various publications, including *Yes!* and the *Chicago Tribune.*

James Howard Kunstler is the author of many books, including *The Long Emergency, The Geography of Nowhere, World Made by Hand,* and *The Witch of Hebron.*

Winona LaDuke is an Anishinaabekwe (Ojibwe) enrolled member of the Mississippi Band Anishinaabeg who lives and works on the White Earth Reservations. She is also the executive director of Honor the Earth, where she works on a national level to advocate, raise public support, and create funding for frontline native environmental groups. Her books include *The Militarization of Indian Country* and *Recovering the Sacred: The Power of Naming and Claiming.*

Bill McKibben is the author of a dozen books about the environment, beginning with *The End of Nature* in 1989, which is regarded as the first book for a general audience on climate change. He is a founder of the grassroots climate campaign 350.org, which has coordinated fifteen thousand rallies in 189 countries since 2009. He is a scholar in residence at Middlebury College.

Janisse Ray is the author of four books of literary nonfiction, including *Ecology of a Cracker Childhood,* and a collection of poetry. A naturalist and activist as well as a writer, she is on the faculty of Chatham University's low-residency MFA program and is a Woodrow Wilson Visiting Fellow.

Rebecca Solnit is the author of thirteen books, including *A Paradise Built in Hell*, *Storming the Gates of Paradise*, and *A Field Guide to Getting Lost*. As an activist and journalist, she has worked on issues such as climate change, Native American land rights, the antinuclear movement, human rights, and other issues.

Sandra Steingraber is an internationally recognized authority on the environmental links to cancer and human health. She is the author of the books *Living Downstream*, *Having Faith*, and *Raising Elijah*. In 2011 she received the Heinz Award and donated the $100,000 prize to the fight against hydrofracking in New York State.

Curtis White is a professor of English at Illinois State University. A novelist and essayist, he has written several widely acclaimed books, including *The Middle Mind: Why Americans Don't Think for Themselves* and *The Barbaric Heart*. His essays have appeared in *Harper's Magazine*, *Playboy*, and *The Village Voice*.

ABOUT ORION MAGAZINE

SINCE 1982, *Orion* has been a meeting place for people who seek a conversation about nature and culture that is rooted in beauty, imagination, and hope. Through the written word, the visual arts, and the ideas of our culture's most imaginative thinkers, *Orion* seeks to craft a vision for a better future for both people and planet.

Reader-supported and totally advertising-free, *Orion* blends scientific thinking with the arts, and the intellectual with the emotional. *Orion* has a long history of publishing the work of established writers from Wendell Berry, Terry Tempest Williams, and Barry Lopez to Rebecca Solnit, Luis Alberto Urrea, and Sandra Steingraber.

Orion is also grounded in the visual arts, publishing picture essays and art portfolios that challenge the traditional definition of "environment" and invite readers to think deeply about their place in the natural world. *Orion*'s website, www.orionmagazine.org, features multimedia web extras including slide shows and author interviews, as well as opportunities for readers to discuss *Orion* articles.

Orion is published bimonthly by The Orion Society, a nonprofit 501(c)3 organization, and is available in both print and digital editions.

Subscribe

Orion publishes six beautiful, inspiring issues per year. To get a free trial issue, purchase a subscription, or order a gift subscription, please visit www.orionmagazine.org/subscribe or call 888/254-3713.

Support

Orion depends entirely on the generous support of readers and foundations to publish the magazine and books like this one. To support *Orion*, please visit www.orionmagazine.org/ donate, or send a contribution directly to *Orion* at 187 Main Street, Great Barrington, MA, 01230.

To discuss making a gift of stock or securities, or for information about how to include *Orion* in your estate plans, please call us at 888/254-3713, or send an e-mail to development@ orionmagazine.org.

Shop

Head to the *Orion* website, www.orionmagazine.org, to purchase *Orion* books, organic cotton t-shirts, and other merchandise featuring the distinctive *Orion* logo. Back issues from the past thirty years are also available.

MORE BOOKS FROM ORION

ORION READERS

Orion Readers collect landmark *Orion* essays into short thematic volumes:

Change Everything Now. A selection of essays about ecological urgency.

Thirty-Year Plan: Thirty Writers on What We Need to Build a Better Future. An eloquent statement on the future of humanity.

Wonder and Other Survival Skills. A collection of thoughtful and inspirational writing on our relationship to the natural world.

Beyond Ecophobia: Reclaiming the Heart in Nature Education, by David Sobel. An expanded version of one of *Orion*'s most popular articles that speaks to those interested in nurturing in children the ability to understand and care deeply for nature from an early age.

Into the Field: A Guide to Locally Focused Learning, by Claire Walker Leslie, John Tallmadge, and Tom Wessels, with an introduction by Ann Zwinger. Curriculum ideas for teachers interested in taking their students out of doors.

Place-Based Education: Connecting Classrooms & Communities, by David Sobel. A guide for using the local community and environment as the starting place for curriculum learning, strengthening community bonds, appreciation for the natural world, and a commitment to citizen engagement.

ORION ANTHOLOGIES

Finding Home: Writing on Nature and Culture from Orion *Magazine,* edited by Peter Sauer. An anthology of the best writing from *Orion* published from 1982 to 1992.

The Future of Nature: Writing on a Human Ecology from Orion *Magazine,* selected and introduced by Barry Lopez. An anthology of the best writing from *Orion* published from 1992 to 2007.

FOR EDUCATORS

Ideal for reading groups and academic course adoption, many *Orion* books are accompanied by a downloadable teacher's guide consisting of key discussion questions. Teacher's guides can be found on the *Orion* website at www.orionmagazine.org/education.

Series design by Hans Teensma,
principal of the design studio Impress
(www.impressinc.com), which has
designed *Orion* since 1998.
The typeface is Scala, designed by Dutch
typographer Martin Majoor in 1990.
Printed by BookMobile.